ROBSON
OF THE OLYMPIC

ROBSON
OF THE OLYMPIC

MOLLIE SANDS

The Society for Theatre Research
1979

© The Society for Theatre Research 1979

Published by The Society for Theatre Research
14 Woronzow Road, London NW8 6QE

ISBN 0 85430 029 5

Printed by the Blackfriars Press Ltd.
Leicester
in 10 pt. on 12 pt. Times

Introduction

When The Society for Theatre Research was founded it was certainly in the minds of those responsible that the interests of the Society and of its publications should extend to all forms of live theatrical entertainment. It is, no doubt, natural that the greater emphasis has been placed upon what is termed the legitimate theatre, but it is fitting that we are now able to publish a work dealing with an actor who could have been a star either on the music hall or in straight character roles and who exercised his genius largely in the world of burlesque and extravaganza. It is, moreover, a particular pleasure for us to be able to offer to a wider public a study that saw its genesis in a lecture delivered to the Society.

We must acknowledge with considerable gratitude a donation from Mr. F. Renad Cooper, which has enabled us to produce this book with a range of illustrations worthy of its subject, and in a form less cabined by the need for economy than is usual with the Society's publications.

GEORGE SPEAIGHT
General Editor of Publications
The Society for Theatre Research

List of Contents

List of Illustrations

Plates with more than one subject are described in the order top left, top right, bottom left, bottom right.

The author expresses her thanks to the following for permission to reproduce illustrations in their possession. To Mrs. José Smith for plate 1; to the executors of the late Miss Kathleen Gent for plate 4; to the British Library for plates 6 and 7; to the National Portrait Gallery for plate 12a; and to the British Theatre Museum for plates 3, 11a, 11b, 12b, 12d. Plates 1 and 4 are from photographs by Alec Lessin. The page from Harwood Cooper's manuscript notebook is reproduced on page 21 by permission of F. Renad Cooper.

Acknowledgements

My first thanks are due to Mr. F. Renad Cooper, not only for the loan of his grandfather's notes which made Robson 'come alive' for me, but also for patiently searching out the date of births, deaths and marriages, as mentioned in the text, and making many helpful suggestions. His encouragement at all stages of the work spurred me on. I am grateful to Barry Duncan for his interest, especially in the early stages, for the loan of playbills and books and for giving much time and trouble to solving some of my problems.

Mrs. José Smith and the late Miss Kathleen Gent, great-grand-daughters of Frederick Robson, very kindly showed me the Mazeppa Cane, the Doulton Wine Jug, the Yellow Dwarf silver Cigar Case, and many family letters and portraits. Their recollections of their grandmother, Robson's daughter Fanny, helped to fill in the background. It was through Messrs. Raymond Mander and Joe Mitchenson that I traced Kathleen Gent, and they also gave up much valuable time to showing me their Robson material.

Mr. Edward Fottrell, executor of E. M. Robson's only descendant, allowed me to see and reproduce important papers concerning Frederick Robson left by his 'nephew' E. M. Robson, including the declarations concerning his paternity. Miss Kathleen Barker and Dr. Jane Stedman have been particularly generous with their time, copying out and sending to me anything they have come across in their own work which they thought likely to interest me.

Mr. George Nash and Mr. Anthony Latham of the Enthoven Collection, British Theatre Museum, patiently answered many difficult questions, as well as providing me with the basic material for a study of Frederick Robson's career — the Olympic playbills.

The specialists who have answered my queries include Dr. Stephen Wyatt (burlesque and extravaganza), Dr. Christopher Murray (Robson in Dublin), Mr. Eric Irvin (Mrs. Alfred Phillips in Australia) and Mr. Harry Greatorex (Nottingham).

I have of course spent much time at the British Library at Bloomsbury and the British Newspaper Library at Colindale. The staff of the London Library have been prompt as usual to send off books which I needed to read at home, however bulky. I must thank Sir Robin Mackworth-Young, KCVO, Assistant Keeper of the Queen's Archives, for allowing me to study the programmes of the Royal Theatricals and Queen Victoria's own playbooks at leisure in the Round Tower of Windsor Castle. I have had help from the librarians and staff of Birmingham, Camden, Canterbury, Faversham, Finsbury, The Guildhall, the London Borough of Tower Hamlets, Margate, Nottingham and Stratford-upon-Avon; and on the other side of the Atlantic from the Theatre Collection of Harvard College Library, the Folger Shakespeare Library, Washington D.C., and the Music Department of the Buffalo and Erie County Library (invaluable information on the various editions of 'Vilikens' and its American versions). Permission to quote letters in the Folger Shakespeare Library and the Enthoven Collection has been acknowledged in the text. I am much indebted to Alec Lessin for coming to the house and taking such pains to get good photographs of the Robson family.

Going back to the beginning I owe my first interest in the Olympic, and consequently in Frederick Robson, to my late husband, Brian Jaquet.

Miss Olive Youngs read the final draft, and made many constructive criticisms for which I am very grateful, and also for her undertaking of the important task of the Index. Mrs. Anne Merriman patiently deciphered all the emendations and alterations, and produced an immaculate typescript.

Finally, I must thank Mr. George Speaight for his suggestions and editing, and for shepherding the book through the press.

Mollie Sands

Hampstead, 1978

Foreword

An actor's triumphs at the best are fleeting. Frederick Robson's fame was great during his lifetime, but died with the generation of those who had seen him.

All students of nineteenth century theatre have heard of his legendary acting in the extravaganzas of Planché and the burlesques of Brough, Burnand and Talfourd, but it is difficult for us to understand the appeal to the Victorians of these productions, and the peculiar style of their star. The adjective 'Robsonian' was used for some years after his death — indeed, as late as 1928 — to describe the abrupt transitions 'from side-splitting humour to heartrending pathos', such as he made in *The Yellow Dwarf, Medea* and others.[1] How far were these transitions original and how far an imitation of Edmund Kean, as some writers suggest? No actor of his generation could escape entirely the influence of Kean. However, Henry Crabb Robinson, who had followed Kean closely and was also a great admirer of Robson, did not make this comparison. Before Robson was born, he expressed himself as tired of Kean's convulsions and sudden starts. When in his old age he saw Robson he described his 'exhibition of passion' as 'quite unique'.[2]

This 'exhibition of passion' and the Robsonian transitions were not the whole of Robson's art. Westland Marston, one of his greatest admirers, never saw him in those flamboyant extravaganza or burlesque parts. George Henry Lewes objected 'to all these desecrations of fine works', and would not venture an opinion on Robson's acting power until he had seen him in a non-burlesque character. When he had done so (in *Plot and Passion*) he described him as a remarkable, a very remarkable actor, and prophesied that it was not as a low comedian nor as a tragedian he would excel but as an actor of Bouffé parts, in which character was represented by truthful details.[3]

In straight parts he was considered an innovator by reason of his sincerity, his attention to detail in gesture, movement, make-up and costume, and his 'realism'. According to Dutton Cook, such a figure as Jem Bags ('ragged, miry, miserable . . . ') had not been seen on the stage before.[4] *The Times'* close account of *Daddy Hardacre* speaks of 'the luxury of detail, the magical transition from one feeling to another', adding that 'nothing was done by way of trick'.[5] Of Titus Tuffin, the showman in *Catching a Mermaid, The Era* said that the 'immense effect produced arose not from over-colouring but from a true and just representation of the real thing'. Westland Marston said that:

Nothing could be more microscopic than his observation of characteristics . . . no performer lived more in the details of his part.[6]

Such art would have been in place at the Prince of Wales's, where a year after his death the Bancrofts initiated a new era of comedy. Squire Bancroft himself said of Robson:

Take him all in all, I think he was the most remarkable actor of those times, perhaps of any time.[7]

In some ways he was ahead of his age.

His material was ephemeral. The numerous 'petites comédies', farces, etc., 'from the French' — *Boots at the Swan, Daddy Hardacre, To Oblige Benson, The Porter's Knot* or *Retained for the Defence* – are as unlikely to be revived as the burlesques or extravaganzas. His only character still in the repertoire is Moses in *The School for Scandal*. Had he lived another seven years he might have created some of the Gilbert and Sullivan parts. Then his interpretations might have been handed down, and still seen at fifth hand in amateur companies up and down the country.

We come near to experiencing his art by reading the accounts and opinions of contemporaries: Dickens, Thackeray, Henry James, Francis Burnand, Clement Scott, John Oxenford, G. H. Lewes, the much older Crabb Robinson and various anonymous journalists can help us to imagine what he was like on the stage. The biographer can only try to show him as his contemporaries saw him.

His contemporaries recognised in him 'genius', which we should probably call 'star quality'. But most of them admitted that his theatrical equipment was limited. Nature had given him an ill-proportioned body — a head too large for his five feet in height and his small hands and feet. His voice was not strong, through throat weakness or faulty production, and he was inclined to force it. He lacked staying power, from poor physical stamina or through his training in the fashionable triple bills of three short plays. Irving said of him that he was great enough to know that he could only be great for three minutes.[8] But this weakness he turned to an asset, producing those famous quick transitions, that 'marvellous electric force', which enabled him to play on his audience 'as though they had been the keys of a piano', 'now convulsing them with laughter . . . now hushing them into awe-struck silence'.[9] George Henry Lewes, in what might be called a minority report, thought he portrayed excitability rather than passion. He never represented emotions in their subsidence, Lewes thought, and his transitions were too rapid. Lewes thought this was a fault he could remedy. As no one else regarded it as a fault, he never tried to remedy it.[10]

In his own special field — comedy, tragi-comedy, extravaganza or burlesque — and in his own theatre, the Olympic, his career might have been an unflawed triumph but for the morbid lack of self-confidence which drove him to seek reassurance in drink. The greater his success, the more he feared failure. Drink ended his career at the age of 42. 'Drunk . . . ill . . . memory fails him . . . kills himself with drink . . . mind becomes affected' — such were the notes his colleague Harwood Cooper made of the last two years.

A writer in *The Kentish Observer* says that during his last illness he wailed repeatedly, 'Oh, my wasted and unprofitable life!', his sick mind dwelling on his shortcomings and on the distresses of the recent past, unconsoled by the memories of the affection in which he had been held by his audiences and his many undoubted triumphs.

James Agate remembers that as a boy of nine — in 1886 — he asked his father at the Sunday dinner-table who was the greatest actor he had ever seen. His father (who had seen Macready, Fechter, Barry Sullivan, Vandenhoff, Salvini and Irving) replied unhesitatingly: 'Little Robson!'.[11]

NOTES TO FOREWORD

[1] H. Chance Newton: *Idols of the Halls*, London 1928.
[2] H. Crabb Robinson: *The London Theatre*, edited Eiluned Brown, London 1966.
[3] G. H. Lewes (and John Forster): *Dramatic Essays*, London 1896.
[4] *Gentlemen's Magazine*, 1882.
[5] *Times*, 27 March 1857.
[6] Westland Marston: *Our Recent Actors*, Vol. II, London 1888.
[7] Squire Bancroft: *The Bancrofts, Recollections of 60 Years*, London 1909.
[8] Seymour Hicks: *Twenty-Four Years of an Actor's Life*, London 1910.
[9] H. Barton Baker: *The London Stage*, Vol. 2, London 1869.
[10] See (3) above.
[11] James Agate: 'On Greatness in Acting', *Sunday Times*, 30 July 1939.

Part I

Brownbill into Robson:
1821-1853

1. *The Stage-struck Child, the Engraver and the Amateur*
Thomas Brownbill, who became Frederick Robson, was born at Margate on 22 February 1821.[1] Frederick was added apparently of his own choice when he married at the age of 21, and for a while he was Thomas Frederick Brownbill, or Thomas Frederick Robson; but once established as an actor he was plain Frederick Robson.

Neither Brownbill nor Robson appears in the baptismal registers of Margate Parish Church. Perhaps his parents belonged to the small but flourishing Wesleyan Methodist community, whose Chapel was rebuilt in Hawley Square in 1810, or to the Baptists, whose new Chapel was built in Cecil Square in 1815. All we know of his father is that he is described as 'Philip Brownbill, deceased, stockbroker' in Thomas Frederick Brownbill's marriage certificate of 1842. The absence of any allusions to this father in recollections of his youth suggests that Frederick Robson wished to forget Philip Brownbill. There are several allusions to his mother, Margaret Brownbill, who lived until 1879 and was buried beside her son at Norwood as 'Margaret Robson'.

Why did he call himself Robson? It is tempting to connect him with other theatrical Robsons; a Robson was associated with Mate in the 1787 Patent of the Margate Theatre; a J. D. Robson, proprietor of the Royal Hotel, Margate, took over the theatre in 1842, toured the neighbourhood, visiting also Ipswich in 1843-1844. A J. Robson 'stage manager from the English Opera House' turns up in Nottingham to produce 'the Pieces' in December 1841 and early 1842. A 'Mr. Robson' performs at Nottingham in January 1846. But Robson is a fairly usual name, unlike Brownbill. The most we can say is that he chose a stage-name which already had theatrical connections. There is a certain mystery about his origins, a mystery which seems to have been deliberately fostered.

His mother brought him up to London when he was six years old and took him to the Coburg Theatre to see *The Youthful Queen* (Charles Shannon), *The Green Dragon* (W. T. Moncrieff) and the anonymous *White Eagle, or Villainy Detected*, which specially impressed the child. In addition, Charles Sloman sang comic songs, and the entertainment was preceded by a 'Grand Movable Panorama of a Voyage by Steam from London to Margate', including 'the Effect of a Rainbow at Sea, and a General View of Margate from the Sea'. This bill was given at the Coburg in the week beginning Monday, 3 November 1828. The visit to the Coburg suggests that Margaret Brownbill had friends or relations in South London.

Back in Margate the stage-struck child saved every penny of his pocket-money and of the occasional presents he received until he was able to buy a toy theatre. He acquired *The Forest of Bondy* in Penny Plain, coloured it himself and invited his friends to a performance in which he spoke all the parts. That he had even 'limited' pocket-money and 'occasional presents' shows that he and his mother were not entirely impecunious. About the same time he used to hang about the stage-door of the Theatre Royal, and talk to Stubbs, the low comedian.[2]

He and his mother must have left Margate for good when he was young enough to discard the Kent accent, since this same accent used so convincingly in *The Porter's Knot* and *Daddy Hardacre* is said to have been picked up during his Whitstable engagement, and is never credited to a Margate birth and upbringing. The mature actor often used cockney, which must have been his 'second language'.

Walter Lacy, in recollections written down some time after Robson's death, recalls helping backstage with a juvenile performance of *Richard III* at the Mile End Assembly Rooms, when Richard was played by

> . . . a boy actor who had been taken to see Edmund Kean. The little Richard with his black wig and scarlet dress, made a miniature resemblance of the great actor, and seemed to have imbibed that wonderful combination of physical impulse and inspiration that characterised the original, especially in the detonating and explosive power. The child's mother, was a little fairy-like creature, at whose house I had previously seen him with his own flaxen ringlets, half asleep, like a Blenheim dog, on the skirts of her velvet gown.[3]

Lacy was writing with hindsight. Many others saw the influence of

Kean in Robson's later acting, and attributed it to a first-hand impression in childhood. Perhaps Mrs. Brownbill and her son visited the Coburg again in the summer of 1831 when Kean played Richard, Lear, Othello and Overreach to a rowdy audience which preferred its favourite Cobham, and said so in no uncertain terms. Or they might have gone to Covent Garden the year before, and seen one of Kean's best Richards.

It is not improbable that Mrs. Brownbill was 'a little fairy-like creature', since her son grew up much under the normal height. His hair remained curly in later years, but a painting of him as a young man in the possession of Mrs. José Smith, his great-granddaughter, shows it as red-gold rather than flaxen (see plate 1).

Some years after this episode Lacy was sitting behind 'a little lady' at the Grecian while Robson was on stage singing 'The Country Fair'. He recognised her as the mother of the little Richard III, but could not remember the name: 'Biffin or Tiffin, or something like that!'. Chester, the Buckingham of the juvenile performance, assured him it was 'Button', which is at least a two-syllabled name beginning with a B.

Mrs. Brownbill and her son were settled in South London by 1836, possibly in Henry Street, Vauxhall. The boy was apprenticed at fifteen to Thomas George Smellie, New Round Court, Bedfordbury, Strand, copperplate engraver and printer of many of Cruikshank's plates, who was at that address in 1836-1840.[4]

The little community of Bedfordbury provided every kind of shop: old furniture shops, sweet shops which displayed in their window-panes strings of farthing and halfpenny literature, key shops selling rusty keys of all types, and a herb shop where a stuffy old man sold stalks and roots for the cure of all human ills. Goodwin's Court still leads from St. Martin's Lane into Bedfordbury, and here some old houses may still be seen, little changed since Robson's day. In the centre paved court a variety of London characters could have been seen, imitated by young Brownbill to the delight of his friends. His later art owed much to his observation of the mannerisms and idiosyncrasies of cockney characters. Like Dickens, he was an adopted not a born Londoner, and perhaps this gave them both an especially keen relish for the special characteristics of the people among whom they came to live.

'Little Bill' dressed showily, wearing a large hat with a twisted brim set jauntily upon his 'artificially curled ringlets'. (We know that these ringlets were natural.) The boys of the Court called him 'Little Big Head', and 'Little Big Head' he remained all his life; he never grew above five feet tall, and his head was too big for his small hands, feet and body.[5]

After four years of the apprenticeship Smellie gave up, and young Robson carried on his own business with some of his master's clients in Brydges Street, spending his evenings at amateur theatres or sing-songs. Smellie's name disappears from street guides after 1840, and that of Thomas Brownbill appears as Copperplate Engraver in Brydges Street. W. Y. Laing says he was a seal engraver of considerable talent, earning enough to appear the 'buck and dandy' among his friends.[6] He was thus a skilled craftsman, enjoying some financial security, upon which he was shortly to turn his back. The 1841 Census shows him living with his mother in Ward Street, Lambeth; they are described as 'not born in this county', and his occupation as 'engraver'.

On 12 May 1842 the young engraver appeared as Simon Mealbag in *Grace Huntley* (H. Holl) at the Little Theatre in Catherine Street, Strand. Catherine Street then formed one thoroughfare with Brydges Street, where he worked. Smythson had taken over the Little Theatre in 1835, and designated it 'The Royal Pantheon'. He would 'sell' parts to aspirants; it cost £5 to play Richard III, whereas Richmond was only £2.10, and so on down the scale. Smythson provided theatre, scenery, costumes and printing.[7] J. A. Cave said he had seen some excellent performances at this little theatre, especially by 'Typos', and many professionals of repute had made their débuts there, such as Leigh Murray and Henry Marston.

But Robson's début was a failure, a fact mentioned in all accounts of his early years, including those sanctioned by himself. Like many successful artists he was probably rather proud of the fact that his early talent was not recognised. Smythson himself had died in 1841, and in 1843 the theatre became a coffee house, so Robson's appearance there must have been in its last year.

He was not discouraged, and one morning — probably towards the end of 1842 — his neighbours in Brydges Street found a paper attached to the shutters announcing that he had given up business. Increasing eye-strain may have influenced his decision. In all his portraits we see small, screwed-up eyes as if he had concentrated on close work for too long. But probably the main reason for his change of direction was an irresistible desire to act.

2. *The Bower Saloon, 'The Country Fair' and Harwood Cooper*

At what point in his early career he appeared at the Bower Saloon, Lambeth, it is difficult to determine — whether before he went on tour in the provinces, or in between tours. Not all writers mention this short but important engagement, and it is possible Robson wished it forgotten.

'The Sour Balloon', as it was often called, started life as the Duke's Arms. This was the time when concert rooms were being added to many London taverns, giving mixed entertainment for local audiences and employment for out-of-work professionals and semi-amateurs. G. A. Hodson, manager of the Bower in the 1840s, was actor, singer, composer and fiddler; he gave his patrons mixed bills of melodrama, ballad opera, sing-songs and fireworks. It was a family affair, and his two talented daughters helped him. He paid his artists from 12/- to £1 weekly. Many of them lived in the nearby Hercules Buildings. *Punch* described the Saloon as rather like a chapel. In front of the seats were ledges which held pewter pots instead of hymn books. The greater part of the audience was 'respectable mechanics', with a good sprinkling of would-be actors.[8, 9] There were no footlights but a series of lights was carried around the proscenium arch, concealed from the audience by 'a very elegant trellis-work supporting a foliage of vine-leaves'. The little theatre was pretty. The stage could be lowered or raised as required, and the actors entered from above or below, not from the wings. A Swiss village scene was permanently built in.

J. Arnold Cave, a buffo bass who sang 'Nigger' songs blacked-up, and comic songs without such disguise, joined the Bower Saloon in 1842, and 'frequently met a little gentleman in front of the theatre whose good-looking and expressive face' attracted him. The little gentleman said his name was Frederick Robson, and here (unless Cave's memory was at fault) we have the first use of the name. He was 'a bit of a mimic' and was going to appear at the little theatre in Catherine Street. He gave Cave some idea of his talents, tilting his hat on the back of his head: 'the whole expression of his face and figure altered; his voice had changed, and when he had finished I could have sworn we were in the presence of Edward Wright, one of the greatest comedians we have ever had'. Cave prophesied a great future for him. Soon after this, 'the little gentleman' joined Hodson's company at the Bower 'playing strongly-marked character parts'.[10]

Robson was impressed by one of Cave's songs, 'The Statty Fair', and added it to his own budget ('Budget' was used of a collection of songs or monologues; 'Bannister's Budget', for instance, was the one-man show with which Jack Bannister at one time toured the country).

The real name of the song was 'The Country Fair', 'Statty' or 'Statue' (as Harwood Cooper calls it) being a corruption of statute. It was first performed by Mr. Mathews in J. B. Buckstone's *The May-queen* in 1828, and is what would have been called a Polylogue.

In an easily-learnt tune within a limited vocal range the singer tells us:

Yes I own 'tis my delight
  To see the laughter and the fright
In such a motley, merry sight
  As a country fair.

Full of riot, fun and noise
  Little girls and ragged boys
The very flower of rural joys
  Is fun beyond compare.

Some are playing single-stick
  Boys in roundabouts so thick
Maidens swinging till they're sick
  All at a country fair.

Wooden toys and lollipops
  Ribbons, lace and shilling hops
Peg and whip and humming tops
  All at a country fair.

Then came the spoken part:

> Oh here we are in the thick of the fair; look at the people, and the shows and the music; Oh I do so like it, Ma! Walk up, walk up, ladies and gentlemen, this is the only booth in the fair where you will see a grand, farcical, tragical, comical play . . . Walk up, walk up and see the grand Shropshire Giant, he is nine foot high, gentlemen . . .

And so on, giving scope for improvisation and business.

It seems to have been first sung out of context in Charles Selby's *Catching an Heiress* in 1835 by J. Reeve as Tom Twig and Baron Sowercrautzen-sausengen, parts later played by Frederick Robson innumerable times. He also introduced it into other entertainments, and indeed it was the song most associated with him, apart from 'Vilikens'.

One of the writers who mentions the Bower Saloon is Harwood Cooper, whose notebook (hitherto unpublished) will be extensively quoted from now on. The present author owes a great debt of gratitude to Harwood Cooper's grandson, F. R. Cooper, not least for the loan of this notebook and permission to quote from it.

From his reference to the Bower it seems likely that Harwood Cooper had already entered Robson's life by this time. Frederick Harwood Cooper, eldest son of Fox Cooper the dramatist, was born in

Robsonian Mems.

a anecdote (printed) of his sheerness engagement with Jackman

1. Bower Saloon. 1842

2. Eccentric Club.. South St-

3. Eagle Tavern & Grecian Saloon.

2 Wenches at Coffee Shop.

Dinners on the Cheap.

3 Ireland. Dublin.

Robson unintentially insults the Audience. "Hypocrite" Mawworm. See Engraving in "Theatrical Times"

"Forbidden Fruit in the garden of Eden aisey wasn't it an apple. reply "I call that "Apple sauce" but if you want to know what fruit it to as ask. Father Doughty Doughderty Had to leave the Theatre

A page from Harwood Cooper's notebook.

21

1826 in Mount Gardens, Lambeth, and baptised in the parish church of St. Mary's. Although in his childhood and youth he must have followed his peripatetic father to various short-stay homes in various parts of London, when he was grown-up he lived in or near Lambeth for the rest of his life, like many other theatre people.[11] Besides those in regular work who found it convenient to walk across Waterloo Bridge to their theatres, there was a floating population of semi-amateurs, out-of-work pros. and aspirants, associated with the Bower, the little Eccentric Club in Hercules Buildings or one of the many South London 'Dukeys', as well as the more seedy 'Penny Gaffs', which presented Shakespeare, performing animals, and singing and dancing in makeshift theatres in back alleys.

From this stratum of Lambeth society came Rosetta May, Robson's wife.

3. *The Stroller and the Married Man*

On 21 September 1842 Thomas Frederick Brownbill, engraver, was married to Rosetta Frances May, spinster, both 'of full age', at the parish church where Harwood Cooper had been baptised. The witnesses were Henry May, 'Gentleman', the bride's father, and Claudius H. M. May, her brother, of Pilgrim Street, Lambeth. It is strange that Mrs. Brownbill was not a witness.

Pilgrim Street was the same sort of street of small houses as Ward Street in which the Brownbills lived. We do not know how Henry May justified his claim to be a gentleman, but Harwood Cooper describes Claudius May as 'the Hamlet', which suggests that he acted at one of the Lambeth theatrical establishments. Claudius was also 'a particular friend' of one of 'the amateurs of the Bower', Shipman, promoter of the little Eccentric Club, and a lifelong friend of Frederick Robson. Did Rosetta also act? Twenty years later she played Creusa to her husband's Medea under the name of Miss Hastings.[12] S. May was a well-known theatrical costumier in the mid-nineteenth century, responsible for some of the costumes at the Olympic. But the name is too common for us to claim him as one of Robson's in-laws. Mrs. Hannah May, who lived at 3 Pilgrim Street in 1849, described as the widow of a farmer, is a more likely connection, in which case the Mays had country roots which might account for Rosetta's skill with baby animals, one of the few pleasant traits recollected by her descendants.

It was possibly soon after his marriage that young Brownbill went off to Whitstable. The theatre was in a private house, and he earned 5/- or 7/- a week. At Faversham, where fishermen helped him rig up a booth, he earned 18/- for three days' acting. He kept two relics of this engagement for many years: the 'best coat' in which he used to sing 'The Country Fair' and a twopenny-halfpenny brooch which a boy had given him in lieu of admission money.[13]

Had young Brownbill-Robson read William Rede's 1835 edition of his brother's *The Road to the Stage,* he would have found a list of provincial circuits and their managers to whom he might make application, with a suggestion that he might employ a theatrical agent to undertake the correspondence for him. He would have also found practical hints as to how to behave in a strange theatre, what costumes to provide and where to buy them, what make-up to use, and some instruction in voice production and acting technique.[14] The description of the hard life of a country actor might have deterred him from seeking his fortune out of London, but the author considered this a far better training than the expensive practice of 'buying' parts in private London theatres.

There are some discrepancies in the various accounts of Brownbill-Robson's strolling days, and chronology is hard to establish, but the general picture is convincing: Jackman's,[15] Rogers', Chester's and Richardson's companies (the last a booth company); Sheerness, Whitehaven and Nottingham; the Kent, Bedford and St. Albans' circuits. He also reached Cornwall, according to James Orlando Watts, uncle of Theodore Watts Dunton. He was 'a little actor who was a real genius', reminding him of what he had read of Kean's acting, in a company of strollers in a vast stone-built barn at St. Ives.[16] Another writer sends him north 'to the provinces of Scotland'.

If he really covered all this territory between quitting his shop towards the end of 1842 and appearing at the Grecian on 12 February 1844 he must have travelled with remarkable speed. Conditions for the stroller were certainly improved since the eighteenth century and many towns were already linked by the railroad. Yet there were still occasions when a company would be literally 'on the road', on foot or helped by horse-and-cart or coach.

Henry Compton (Robson's predecessor at the Olympic), Chippendale (later of the Haymarket, and a friend of Robson's) and William Robertson (Dame Madge Kendal's father) once had to walk 30 miles with only five shoes between them; they took it in turn to walk with one shoe.

The only engagement impossible to account for is Nottingham. There are good records of the Nottingham Theatre for 1842-1844, but there is no mention of a Robson or Brownbill, except the J. Robson mentioned earlier.[17] Yet Rouse advertised his first appearance at the

Grecian as 'from the Nottingham Theatre', and when Harris of the Theatre Royal, Dublin, listed the ladies and gentlemen engaged for the 1852-1853 season he described Robson (already well-known in Dublin) as 'from the Theatre Royal, Nottingham'. Perhaps both Rouse and Harris assumed that J. Robson and Frederick Robson were one and the same. It was good publicity, and perhaps Frederick Robson was willing to overlook the inaccuracy.

At Christmas 1843 he returned to London because of ill-health, and on his recovery proceeded to two unlucky engagements, Tunbridge Wells and the Standard. Just before Christmas, on 17 December, his son Frederick Henry was born at the May home in Pilgrim Street, but not registered until 12 January 1844. ('Henry' was presumably after his paternal grandfather).

On 12 February 1844 there appeared at 'the Eagle Saloon and Grecian Theatre' for the first time:

Mr. Robson from the Nottingham Theatre
in
The Wags of Windsor

But Thomas Frederick Brownbill, engraver, survived side by side with Mr. Robson, comedian, for at least two years. The birth certificate of his daughter Frances, on the 26 July 1846 in Great Chart Street, describes her father as Thomas Frederick Brownbill, engraver, with no mention of his theatrical employment at the nearby Grecian.

He was 23, and perhaps Mrs. José Smith's portrait was painted about this time. As time went on, the face took on lines of humour and lines of strain, and the eyes became heavy-lidded. In photographs the hair looks dark, and sometimes rather damp. Perhaps he dyed it because its colour was too conspicious for the stage.

4. *The Grecian: Jack of All Trades*

Harold Scott calls the Grecian 'a cockney Arcadia'.[18] There were indoor theatrical entertainments and concerts, and in fine weather outdoor concerts, with balls and fireworks. Mr. Rouse, proprietor in Robson's time, gave his patrons fashionable comedies, Italian opera, ballet, promenade concerts and 'incidentals' — solo songs by singers and comedians as *entr'actes,* or after the main entertainment. The audience was predominantly middle-class and respectable. A few years later J. E. Ritchie remarked that it was not 'the fast men' but the family audiences which made the establishment pay.[19]

24

Another use made of these north London gardens testifies to their respectable character: the Benefits for various Friendly Societies. The avowed purpose of these Societies was the cultivation of thrift and prudence, as well as the succour of members who had fallen on hard times. Some of the smaller Societies indulged in rather too much beer and tobacco, but on the whole they 'operated powerfully to hold Victorian society together'.[20] The Societies for which Benefits were held during Robson's time included the Slop and Army Cutters' Vacation Fund, the Pocket Book and Leathermakers' Pension Society, and the Friendly Society of Copperplate Printers. This last must surely have appealed to Robson.

How did he get this engagement? Hollingshead says he was 'recommended' by Milano the ballet-master when there was a vacancy for a low comedian. How Milano knew Robson is not stated. Besides being ballet-master this gentleman was in charge of the confectionery department, and Boucicault said there was 'a tradition' that Robson was first engaged as a waiter.[21] Bridgeman says the young man was about to set off for the country again with a heavy heart when Mr. Rouse sent for him to 'go on and dance in ballets' and 'to do anything that was required'.[22, 23]

This included Justice Shallow in *The Merry Wives of Windsor*, with Campbell (the 'heavy') as Falstaff, and young Bailey in an adaptation of *Martin Chuzzlewit* with Campbell doubling Pecksniff and Sarah Gamp. (Later Robson himself was to give a Sarah Gamp Monologue.) He also played a number of 'bit' parts in opera: Christie in Barnett's *The Mountain Sylph*, Velasquez in Auber's *The Duc d'Olonne*, and Daniel in Adolphe Adam's *Le Chalet*, among others. In a 'ballet d'action' called *Star of Eve*, 'invented' by Mr. Deulin, he played Jeanne, a character part. The dancing which was to be important in his extravaganza performances was probably acquired under the tutelage of Milano or Deulin. The classical ballets performed by members of the Leclerq family may have suggested features in his Taglioni imitation of 1856.

More important for his future was Wormwood in *The Lottery Ticket*, by Samuel Beazley junior, with Miss M. A. Crisp and Mr. Dixon. It has been said that he played opposite 'Johnson', the future Sims Reeves, in this farce at the Grecian. Wormwood is a thoroughly unpleasant character. A hunchbacked lawyer's clerk, a mischief-maker and a busybody, he delights in setting everybody by the ears: 'What puppets they are, and I am the showman!' Hollingshead said Robson played Wormwood as it had never been played, unless by Edmund Kean.[24] In Wormwood perhaps we see Desmarets, the Yellow Dwarf and Prince Richcraft in embryo. There was a sinister side to Robson's art, in sharp contrast to the whimsical and endearing.

A Spanking Legacy (T. G. Blake) and *Popping the Question* (J. B. Buckstone) came into his repertory about this time, and also Lenville in H. Horncastle's adaptation of *Nicholas Nickleby*. In the 'spectacular production' of *The Maid and the Magpie* (possibly the N. Lee version) he had the part of 'a bustling old lady', and his name in large type. Benjamin Bowbell in *Illustrious Stranger* (J. Kenney and J. Millingen) was an early Grecian success, repeated in Dublin but not at the Olympic. Hollingshead and his friend Moy Thomas were at the first night, and Hollingshead said that from that night Robson never looked back. This so-called 'operatic farce', about a little man wrecked on the shores of China, who finds himself caught up in various palace intrigues including betrothal to the Princess, gave him one of those bewildered-little-man parts which he was to play with such success. Timid, rather cowardly, not very intelligent, this was to be Lancelot Briggs in *Ticklish Times,* Pawkins in *Retained for the Defence,* Benjamin Bobbin in *B.B.*, Hugh de Brass in *A Regular Fix* and others. These characters seem to anticipate Ko Ko faced with carrying out an execution, Robin Oakapple trying to be a Bad Bart., and other Gilbertian figures, played after Robson's death by George Grossmith.

The document of Robson's 1847 're-engagement' by Rouse for a further year from 11 May was preserved by E. M. Robson and reproduced by Burnand.[25] His salary was £3 per week playhouse pay, out of which he had to provide his own costumes, but he earned as much as £50 at a Benefit. On 13 May Robson scored a big success in the travestie part of Jenny Lind in *More Ethiopians, or Jenny Lind in New York* (Mr. Campbell).

The fashion for Nigger Minstrels, or Burnt Cork Minstrels, was a curious phenomenon of mid-nineteenth century popular entertainment. The first, Jim Crow Rice, had based his act on the grotesque singing and dancing of a negro ostler, but the troupes of Nigger Minstrels which began to invade England in the 1830s had little connection with genuine negro folk music. There was a flood of tuneful songs by composers both American and English, which were made into minstrel songs by the substitution of 'dis', 'dat', and 'ole' for 'this', 'that' and 'old'. As an article in *The Train* for 1857 says, sober spinsters were heard to lapse into the pathetic plaint of a Sukey or a Dinah of home manufacture. The best of the composers were Stephen Foster, Christy of the Christy Minstrels, and Dam Emmett, whose Virginian Minstrels were popular in the States in 1843, and for whom he wrote 'Dixie'. After 1864 a generally pro-South English public regarded these songs as Confederate.

But London in general and the Grecian in particular were far from such thoughts in 1847. The ballet *Boatmen of the Ohio* had been a great success for two months. Mr. Deulin's performance as Old Joe was 'stamped as one of the most finished and original performances ever witnessed', with music composed of 'Nigger' melodies. This Grecian success, combined with that of the 'Ethiopian Serenaders' at the Hanover Square Rooms in January 1846, inspired Mr. Rouse to commission an 'Ethiopian Sketch' by Mr. Campbell. Mr. Campbell cleverly exploited the craze for Jenny Lind combined with the craze for nigger minstrels, and gave his audience two topical features for the price of one. He also gave the principal low comedian a good travestie part as Jenny Lind. As well as impersonating the Swedish Nightingale, Robson had to learn to play 'the bones' and to produce the patter traditionally associated with the gentleman who played that instrument in a nigger troupe, and was himself known as 'The Bones'.

On Friday, 14 May, Mr. Rouse announced that *More Ethiopians* was received with 'shouts of acclamation and applause', while Mr. Robson's personation of Jenny Lind convulsed the audience with laughter. His performance on the bones 'stamped him a first-rate professor'. A few days later the sketch was described as 'one of the most decided hits ever made within the walls of a theatre'. The melodies, 'perfectly harmonised, were sung by *twenty,* under the direction of Mr. Baldwin'.

Robson learnt to play not only the bones that season, but also the drum as Georges Batteur in *The Daughter of the Regiment*.

On 31 August, for the Benefit of the Philanthropic Knights of St. James's, he sang 'The Gravesend Packet', and shared the bill with Charles Sloman, one of the great serio-comics of the old tavern concerts, whom he must have heard as a child when he visited the Royal Coburg in 1827. 'The Improvisatore Inglese' as he called himself was a figure from the past, from the Cider Cellars and the Coal Hole in their heyday, and his appearances in the 1840s were few. Yet there must have been something of the old power remaining from the days when he held his audiences spellbound with ballads such as 'The Maid of Judah', composed by himself, or Shield's 'The Wolf'. Young Robson may well have picked up some ideas which helped him to build up his own serio-comic style.

Rouse recorded in October 1847 that 'all the pieces produced lately have been most enthusiastically received'. Robson's share was comedy or farce. 'Roars of laughter and shouts of irresistible applause' greeted *Our Wife* (T. Archer), in which he played opposite O'Donnell.

27

Throughout *A Mistaken Story* (T. E. Wilks), in which he played Mr. Piccanniny to Annette Mears' Seraphina, 'there was a continual strain of laughter'. This remained in his repertoire, but more important for his future was his first appearance as Jacob Earwig in Selby's *Boots at the Swan*, which 'convulsed the audience from first to last'. That year also saw his first Jerry in *A Day after the Fair*, in which he impersonated Sam Wax the Cobbler, Susan Squall the old ballad-singer, Mademoiselle Dumplino and Timothy Thumpwell, the drummer. This farce by C. A. Somerset remained a *tour de force*, and was to be the cause of the celebrated 'incident' which banished him from Dublin (see below).

In December he was Moses in *The School for Scandal*, another part he was to play frequently, with Annette Mears as Lady Teazle, and in April 1848 he appeared in *Robson's Academy*, a kind of one-man show written for him by Mr. Campbell. By the middle of 1848 he was sufficiently established to have the short Memoir published in the *Theatrical Times* (19 August 1848), accompanied by his portrait as Mawworm in *The Hypocrite* (I. Bickerstaffe).

5. *The Comic Singer*

Understandably nothing is said in the Memoir about his comic singing in the 'Incidentals', in the Hall of Nations or in the Gardens. Among his solo songs were: 'Lord Lovel', 'The Lost Child', 'The Gravesend Packet', 'Going to Greenwich by Water' and (if we are to believe some writers) 'Vilikens and his Dinah'. The problem of 'Vilikens' is discussed in the Appendix. 'The Country Fair', acquired by him at the Bower, was first sung by him at the Grecian in February 1847 in *Sketches in India* (anon.). At the end of February he introduced it into Selby's *Catching an Heiress,* the context in which it remained most familiar. The following year he added 'the burlesque cachucha'.

Hollingshead says that his fame as a singer spread over North London. Club 'Free and Easies' at Dalston and elsewhere engaged him on Sunday evenings for a guinea and refreshments:

> This was the Robson known only to a select few at the West End of London — the Charles Dickens and Alfred Smith groups, who were always going outside the conventional bounds in search of talent.[26]

Dr. G. L. M. Strauss regretted that Robson had not received the benefit of an intelligent dramatic education instead of 'having to make his way through the tap-rooms and bar parlours of public houses'.[27] Free-and-easies, tap-rooms and bar parlours . . . the mention of such

28

Plate 1. Robson as Jem Bags, 1853.

Plate 2. 'Villikins and his Dinah' as published in the Musical Bouquet.

PRICE ONE SHILLING.

THE

LEGEND

OF

Wilikind Dinah

Illustrated by George Thompson.

London:—
TALLANT AND ALLEN, 21, WARWICK SQUARE, PATERNOSTER ROW.

Plate 3. An edition of 1854, showing Robson on stage as Jem Bags.

Plate 4. The Olympic Theatre. Exterior and interior, 1849.

places would have caused much distress to those of Robson's friends who thought even 'music hall' derogatory.

After success of this type, why did not Robson turn his back upon aspirations to be a legitimate actor, and make a career in Song and Supper Rooms, as did his great contemporary, Sam Cowell, the hero of Evans's? Whatever his friends said, he certainly had his music hall side. Even in his great days at the Olympic he was content to step out alone before the curtain and enthral his audiences with 'Vilikens' or 'The Country Fair', with apparently no sense that it was *infra dig.*

But this was not the whole of Robson. A music hall artist must be self-sufficient, must make his impact quickly, without other actors, props or scenery to help him. Robson could do this brilliantly, but clearly it did not fully satisfy him. The true music hall artist has the limitations of his self-sufficiency; he does not play happily into the hands of others, nor they into his. The true actor needs others, and is inspired by them. Robson was a true actor, and at times even a good ensemble actor.

What was his singing like? We hear little about his singing voice; probably it was a typical comedian's, unremarkable in range or volume, and possibly marred by the same huskiness as his speech. But what he did with that voice was remarkable.

M. Willson Disher thinks he was one of the first to bring to cockney humour 'a high genius of interpretation'.[28] Mr. Disher tries to define the cockney spirit, with its mockery of fine feelings, its guying of tragedy. Cockney or not, there is a black humour in many of these songs: take 'Lord Lovel', sung by both Robson and Cowell:

> Then he flung himself down by the side of the corpse
> With a shivering gulp of a guggle,
> Gave two hops, three kicks, blew his nose
> Sung a song, then died in the struggle.

There is a foretaste of *The Mikado* in this, and indeed the charge of cruelty levelled at W. S. Gilbert could be levelled equally at many comic song-writers of this period.

A later, non-cockney example is 'My Dog Tray', sung by Robson in *Masaniello*:

> But in those mutton pies
> Methinks I recognise
> The flavour of my poor dog Tray.

Mr. Willson Disher praises, too, 'the high-spirited flamboyance of cockney speech' and the extra vowels which give such colour to songs like 'Vilikens', as in the following verse:

Now as Dinah vas a valikin in the garding one day
 The father comed up to her and thus did he say
Go dress yourself Dinah in gor-ge-ous array
 And I'll bring you home a husiband both galliant and gay.

The incidental songs in the extravaganzas and burlesques are in a different category. Musically, they are pastiches, and dramatically they are part of the plot, although Robson introduced into them many of his own touches, including cockney speech and an occasional burlesque dance.

During the second half of 1848 and the following year, old successes were repeated and new ones added. It must have been a happy time. He was gradually learning his power to make people laugh, even though he could not yet play upon their emotions 'as on the strings of a piano'. Indeed, he told Harwood Cooper that he was happier in those Grecian days than at the peak of his fame at the Olympic, when he was haunted by a fear of failure.

The Cooper family had moved to North London about the time Robson went to the Grecian. Harwood described himself at this period as 'Professor of Elocution'. In his notes about this period of Robson's life, under the heading 'Eagle Tavern and Grecian Saloon', he writes: 'Two wenches at coffee shop. Dinners on the cheap'. This conjures up a picture of two impecunious young actors ingratiating themselves with the ladies behind the bar in order to get a free meal.

Fleetwood says that Robson was friendly with Sam Lane at the Britannia in those days, and when he felt he needed a rise he would get Sam to write to him offering him another 10/-; this offer he would show to Rouse, who would pay the extra 10/- rather than lose him.[29]

Robson was becoming known by 1848-1849. William Davidge says he recommended him to the lessee of Drury Lane at this period. 'Wouldn't have him if he came for nothing!' was the reply.[30] Such was the attitude of the Patent Theatres to the Minors. An 'esteemed friend' of the writer of an *Illustrated London News* article of 16 August 1857 said he made himself an intolerable nuisance by 'boring us' to go and see 'a little man up at the Eagle who would take the shine out of them all one of these days'. At a later stage the 'esteemed friend' went to the Olympic six nights a week, boasting to all that he had been the first to discover Robson's genius.

6. *Theatre or Music Hall?*

In retrospect, the Grecian engagement seems to have been a step forward for the young actor. At least it gave him a certain security, as well as experience of all kinds of parts. But two years after his death certain of his professional friends compared the status of this engagement unfavourably with that of the hand-to-mouth existence of a strolling player. They were giving evidence at an Inquiry into Theatrical Licensing before a Committee of the House of Commons, extensively reported in the April-May *Era,* 1866.[31] The 1843 Act had liberated the Minors and allowed them to take up the full dramatic licence, provided they did not serve refreshments in the auditorium, or allow smoking. The Bower, the Eagle Saloon, the Grecian Theatre and many others had evolved from the old Saloon or Long Room, in which refreshments were served during the performance, and which had no dramatic licence for the spoken drama. Opera and ballet were therefore strongly represented at such places. After the 1843 Act those houses which did not take up the full dramatic licence developed in the course of time into Music Halls.

The Eagle Saloon, Grecian Theatre, undoubtedly took up the full licence. In February 1844, however, when Robson first appeared there, it is doubtful if all the facilities for refreshments and smoking had been removed. Therefore it was debatable whether Robson's earliest successes were gained in a proper theatre or in a Music Hall. Evidence was given by several actors who had known him personally. Most were anxious to protect his memory from the stigma of having performed in a Music Hall, or its equivalent; the term did not come into general use until the 1850s. The test was: were there still ledges for drinks in front of the seats, and was smoking allowed?

John Hollingshead lived near the Grecian and was about 17 when Robson first appeared there. He maintained that there was drink and tobacco smoke in February 1844, but that the standard was high with 'very perfect performances'. Robson there performed most of the characters which later made him famous at the Olympic, and he was 'full of art' before he went to Dublin. Indeed, the Queen's at Dublin was a very rough house, which charged only 3d for the half-price pit, whereas the Grecian charged 6d; thus Hollingshead.

But J. B. Buckstone refused to give the Grecian any credit for Robson's later successes. He had to go to a *theatre*, i.e. Dublin, to earn the reputation which afterwards carried him to the Olympic.

Benjamin Webster took the same line: Robson was not yet a great actor at the Grecian. In a Music Hall, acting talent would retrogress, whereas a strolling player could learn much: 'Elliston looked on barns as the hot-beds of genius'. Elliston had begun in a barn, so had he himself. A barn might be patronised by local gentry, but those who frequented Music Halls were 'very doubtful people'. After a time at the Queen's, Robson had moved to the Theatre Royal, Dublin, which had an aristocratic audience. Webster clearly considered the social status of the audience an important factor in the training of an actor.

Dion Boucicault was on the side of Hollingshead: Robson *had* learnt his art at the Grecian. Moreover, he had first been engaged as a waiter there. *The Era* printed a letter from Frederick Robson the younger, dated 8 May 1866, protesting that Mr. Boucicault's 'waiter' story was simply not true. His father was a well-educated actor long before Rouse engaged him. Boucicault replied from Paris on 16 May that there was 'a tradition' in the theatrical world that Robson was engaged as an attendant, when Milano the ballet-master was in charge of the confectionery department. He thought such antecedents would have been a cause of pride. W. Y. Laing also wrote a denial of the waiter legend on 6 July 1866, but could not see that it would have been any disgrace.

Horace Wigan emphatically denied that Robson was the product of music halls, and maintained that the Grecian was already a theatre when he first appeared there: the slabs and tables had been put outside. He was already 'a regularly educated actor', who had gone through 'all the miseries of the early part of an actor's career'. By 'regularly educated', Horace Wigan meant experienced, and he gave a list of Robson's provincial engagements.

W. Y. Laing's view differed from that of all Robson's other friends. He maintained that Robson learnt his stage business at the Bower under Hodson, and at the Catherine Street Theatre. At the Grecian he was too noisy, bustling and restless, because he had to play down to his audience. Nor did he show remarkable promise in Dublin. Laing had found great fault with his acting in *The Iron Chest* (G. Colman the Younger) at the Queen's, but Atkins, the low comedian, had prophesied that he would make some of the great ones shake in their shoes. The truth of this was not seen till after his return from Dublin, when 'the fire within him thoroughly kindled up'. The allusion to the Bower — an undoubted Saloon, almost a Dukey — cannot have pleased Robson's friends who were so anxious to protect his reputation from any taint of music hall.

H. J. Turner, theatrical agent, confirmed that the Grecian was a theatre in February 1844. It would have been *infra dig* for an actor to appear in a music hall; *actors* were never recruited from such places.

The Inquiry evidence is inconclusive as to the Grecian's status in 1844, but is very illuminating on the attitudes of the theatrical profession to the music hall in 1866.

Perhaps the truth about Robson is that he learnt something from all his varied experiences, and that during those years his style was slowly maturing.

7. Dublin: The Queen's; The Royal and the Incident

According to Fleetwood, William Farren saw Robson at the Grecian, thought he would be an asset to his own company and arranged for him to go to Dublin to get the experience and status of a legitimate theatre.

True or not, Robson went to the Queen's Theatre, Dublin, in October 1850. This involved changes in his domestic life. His wife Rosetta did not go with him; she stayed with the children 'because of his provincial engagements and other reasons which I need not here state' (see Appendix). These reasons may have included another man in her life or another woman in his.

Robson made his first appearance in Dublin at the Queen's Theatre, Brunswick Street, on 30 October 1850 and his last at the Theatre Royal, Hawkins Street, on 12 March 1853 — the last, that is, until his star 'guest appearances'. During that time he played about 150 parts, long and short, of which eleven or so were already familiar from Grecian days. 'About' is a necessary qualification, since many of the newspaper advertisements lack cast lists, especially at the Queen's. When Harris took over the Royal, he seems to have spent more on publicity.

The Queen's had been built and opened in 1844 by John Charles Joseph, a former chef. After some unfortunate experiences, he sublet it to John Harris on a weekly tenancy. The capable Harris, supported by his wife and leading lady (the former Julia Nichol) collected a good company, and had made a success of the theatre by the time Robson joined, replacing H. Bedford as low comedian.

In the first month Robson established himself as Jerry Ominous in *A Thumping Legacy* (J. M. Morton), Jacob Earwig in *Boots at the Swan* (Charles Selby), Augustus Thistledown in *A Platonic Attachment* (W. B. Bernard), Jerry with 'five other characters' in *A Day after the Fair* (C. A. Somerset) and Daedalus in *Theseus and Ariadne,* his first Planché part. Daedalus was a kind of chorus, and in no way foreshadowed the parts Planché was to write for Robson at the Olympic. The play ran for a month in a double or triple bill which usually included a 'Robson farce'. The ballet with Mademoiselle St. Ouin and Mr. Reynolds as the stars and, during the winter, 'Mons. Desarens and his histrionic dogs and Monkeys' successfully shared the evening, and Robson was lucky enough to have them to boost his first Benefit in

February 1851.

After an Easter recess old favourites were revived and some new parts were given to Robson, notably Master Thomas Smallbones, the only male part in the burletta *The Light Troop at St. James's* (anon.) (set in the Court of Queen Anne); Abd el Kader in a burlesque of *Richard Coeur de Lion;* and Antony in an Interlude of *Antony and Cleopatra* — the last two with Charlotte Saunders (a future Olympic colleague). There is no indication that he showed any special originality in these burlesques. On 17 June he gave a one-man show, *Seeing Robson.*

John Charles Joseph ejected Harris in June 1851, jealous of his success, according to Mrs. Withers the Wardrobe Mistress.[32] He kept on most of Harris's excellent company, including Charlotte Saunders and Robson. *A Mistaken Story* (T. E. Wilks) with Robson as Mr. Piccanniny was given 'for the first time at this theatre'; it had been a Grecian success. The ejected Harris was negotiating for the Royal. This took some time, as arrears of rent were owing to the original lessors, Trinity College.

In October Robson appeared in Planché's *Prince Charming, or the Blue Birds of Paradise* as King Henpeckt the Hundredth with Julia St. George (another future Olympic colleague) as Princess Florian and Fanny Reeves as Prince Charming the First. The scenery was 'entirely new' painted by Mr. Parker, with dresses, properties and decorations 'very splendid'. Robson and Julia St. George were colleagues also in the melodrama, *Flowers of the Forest* (J. B. Buckstone).

A useful experience was Lancelot Gobbo to the Shylock of Sydney Davis. Davis also appeared as Rob Roy with Robson as Bailie Nicol Jarvie; this had been one of Liston's parts also. One wonders what the Scots accent of this Cockney from Kent was like. More suitable was Leporello in *Giovanni in London*, with Fanny Reeves in Vestris's old part.

By the end of 1851 Harris had finally resolved his difficulties and opened on Boxing Night. He had only three weeks in which to engage his company and prepare the holiday programme. Robson and most of the old company joined him. As Tony Nettlethorp in Boucicault's *Love in a Maze* (J. Atkinson) he was received with 'enthusiastic plaudits', and the *Freeman's Journal* of 9 January 1852 described his speciality as this 'peculiar walk of broad comedy' in which Bedford alone (his predecessor) exceeded him. He had no part in the pantomime *Bluff King Hal,* in which his old Grecian colleague, Deulin, was the Harlequin, but on the last night he contributed to the Benefit of Harlequin (Deulin), Clown (Seymour) and Pantaloon (Johnson).

In January 1852 there were four Grand Juvenile Nights, the fourth of which gave Robson his first experience of viceregal splendour, since it was 'By Desire, and under the Patronage of the Lord Lieutenant and the Countess of Clarendon' who brought their own young people. He was playing in *Serve him right* (M. Barnett and C. J. Mathews) with Granby, Webster and Miss Marston (yet another future Olympic colleague). This was followed by the pantomime.

Soon after the end of the pantomime's run, a Grand Fairy Extravaganza, *The Sleeping Beauty in the Wood* (Planché), made its appearance: Robson was the Baron Factotum, Miss Marston the Fairy Antidota, and Miss Julia Harland the Princess Is-a-belle. In the same bill would appear either *Your Life's in Danger* (J. M. Morton), in which he kept the house in 'continual peals of laughter', or *Tender Precautions* (T. J. Serle), which brought him out 'in his richest and happiest vein of humour'. *Seeing Robson* was revived.

After Easter yet another 'fairy extravaganza' was produced: *The Prince of Happy Land* (J. R. Planché), with Robson as the Duke of Vert and Venison, Emma Stanley as Felix and Miss Saunders as Floretta.

Rivalry between the Queen's and the Royal was keen. The Royal was the more aristocratic in general estimation. Sydney Davis had remained at the Queen's and Harris replaced him with T. C. King from Edinburgh. The Queen's gave *The Corsican Brothers* (Boucicault) with Sydney Davis, to which the Royal replied with T. C. King in the same part. Phelps played Macbeth at the Queen's, T. C. King at the Royal. Thus Robson had an opportunity to get to know both *The Merchant of Venice* and *Macbeth* really well, which was perhaps why his later interpretations of the Talfourd burlesques on these plays showed him 'really aware of the tragic foundation'.[33] *Flowers of the Forest* was revived at both houses simultaneously. John Rouse was billed as Jem Bags in *The Wandering Minstrel* at the Queen's. The Royal retorted with Robson as Jem Bags — and so on.

When he had his first Benefit at the Royal on 21 June 1852, his address was given as 13 Creighton Street. The programme included the drama, *The Round of Wrong* (W. B. Bernard) (Robson, King, Granby, Parker, Mrs. Kirby and Mrs. Parker); *Mother and Child are doing well* (J. M. Morton) (Robson as Felix Fluffey); and *Going to the Derby* (J. M. Morton) with Charlotte Saunders, Hurlstone and Webster. His contributions to other actors' Benefits were sometimes in the form of one of his specialities, sometimes in something he might never play again, such as Foxey Jackson in *Eiley O'Connor* (J. T. Haines).

The star billing at the beginning of July was given to Kate and Ellen

Bateman, 'the youthful American artists', who played Shakespearean scenes. The evening usually ended with a Robson farce.

Before the opening of the 1852-1853 season, Harris listed 'the ladies the gentlemen' who had been engaged, 'from' the Theatres Royal in England or Scotland, although most were already known to Dublin audiences. King, Webster and Haigh were from the Theatre Royal, Edinburgh; and Robson, Bromley and Hamilton from the Theatre Royal, Nottingham. As we have seen, Robson's claim to that honour was dubious.

The Queen's opened first: Vandenhoff and Sydney Davis were in *Feudal Times* (G. Colman the younger) and J. L. Toole was giving his version of 'Robson parts'. J. L. Toole recalled that Robson was 'very kind to him', gave him hints and took an interest in everything he did. He came to know him well, and took tea with him. It has been said that Toole took Robson's place in Dublin. This may have been so in the sense that he played the same parts, and possibly inherited some of Robson's popularity. But Toole remained at the Queen's until his farewell on 7 July, three months after Robson left the Royal.

Harris had been 'besought to revive the classic drama' when he took over the Royal, and he responded by opening the 1852-1853 season with *The Winter's Tale*. Bromley was Polixenes; King, Leontes; and Robson, Autolycus. The bill was completed by a Robson farce, *Friend Waggles* (J. M. Morton).

After a week of *The Winter's Tale* there followed one of Harris's most ambitious efforts: *A Midsummer Night's Dream* on 8 November. King was Theseus; Charlotte Saunders, Puck; Miss Lanza, 'from the Princess's', Oberon; George Vining, Lysander; Robson, Bottom the Weaver; and the cast was completed by the ladies St. George and Marston. There were eighteen consecutive performances, usually followed by a Robson farce.

It was revived on 16 December for a Command Performance in the presence of the Lord Lieutenant and the Countess of Eglinton, who had replaced the Clarendons on the change of Ministry. No Lord Lieutenant since the Duke of Northumberland had kept up the Vice-regality in such style. His hospitality, genial manners and interest in the turf made him popular with the upper classes. *The Freeman's Journal* thought it doubly gratifying to find 'the highest personages in the land ratifying by their presence and approval the solid judgement and taste of the lessee in producing the Shakespearean drama'. Nothing had been omitted 'in the items of scenery, music, dresses, decorations etc to give the good acting he has provided its full force and effect'.

Their Excellencies arrived, accompanied by a numerous suite, attended by the usual guard of honour. These command performances with their pomp and ceremony must have been a new experience for the comedian from the provinces, the Bower and the Grecian, and may have helped to prepare him for Queen Victoria's visits to the Olympic, and his own visits to Windsor. But it seems that the Eglintons maintained greater state than Her Majesty.

Nobility and gentry frequently visited the Dublin theatres, their presence duly recorded by the press. Robson was therefore becoming accustomed to an audience less predominantly middle-class than he had known in England. But he had to reckon with the Dublin Gods also, and in some ways they were more difficult than their cockney equivalent. It was the Gods, the Catholic Gods, whom he offended in the INCIDENT.

It seems possible that there was more than one 'incident', since Harwood Cooper's version, presumably derived from Robson, does not tally with that of Mrs. Withers, the Wardrobe Mistress. Harwood Cooper says that Robson unintentionally insulted the audience in *The Hypocrite* when, as Mawworm, he spoke of forbidden fruit in the Garden of Eden, suggesting they should ask Father Dougherty if that fruit were an apple or not. Now Mawworm does not seem to have been a Dublin part, although Robson had played it with success at the Grecian: nor is there in the published text any allusion to the forbidden fruit of the Garden of Eden. It seems unlikely that Harwood Cooper could have invented Father Dougherty and the apple, but he might have confused this with some other play.

The most plausible account of the Dublin incident comes from Mrs. Withers.[34] As Jerry in *A Day after the Fair* Robson appeared as a drunken cobbler who sings 'I've been drinking, I've been drinking' to the tune of 'I've been roaming', and then says 'Formerly I was a preacher (or parson), but latterly I've left off all my evil ways (hiccup) though I still continue to be a mender of soles'. According to Mrs. Withers, Robson made a bet that he would substitute the word 'priest' for 'preacher' or 'parson': which he did, and brought down the wrath of the Gods on his head, causing Harris to dismiss him.

A Day after the Fair (C. Somerset) was played on 5 January 1853, after which Robson disappeared from the bills for a fortnight. This seems more like suspension than dismissal. On 19 January he reappeared, and remained until the end of the season.

Before the incident he had played some odds and ends, including Tony Lumpkin, Filch *(Beggar's Opera)*, Billy Lackaday in *Sweethearts and Wives* (J. Kenney) and Solomon in *The Quaker* (C. Dibdin).

During the seven or eight weeks after his return and before the end of the season, he played in one new farce, *A Phenomenon in a Smock Frock* (W. Brough) as John Buttercup, a milkman, as well as in various revivals, such as *Illustrious Stranger, The Critic, The Rivals* and *Mischiefmaking* (J. B. Buckstone). On 22 February he was Sampson Rawbold in *The Iron Chest* (G. Colman the younger), followed by Jem Bags in *The Wandering Minstrel,* in which he was billed to sing 'an original Legend, entitled VILLIKIND AND HIS DINAH'.

His last night as a salaried performer at the Theatre Royal was 12 March 1853, when the bill included *The Rivals* and *Mischiefmaking* (Nicholas Dovetail). Even if he had not offended the Gods, Robson might well have been ready to leave Dublin. Levey and O'Rourke say he left because he was refused a small increase in salary, and this may have been a contributory factor.[35]

J. L. Toole says he was with Robson when he received an offer from Farren to play at the Olympic, and that he saw him off to England.[36]

NOTES TO PART I

[1] 1822 is sometimes given, but he was described as 'of full age' in the marriage certificate of 21 September 1842, and 43 on the death certificate of 12 August 1864. Margate was given as his place of birth in accounts of his life 'derived from his own lips', such as that in *The Theatrical Times* of 19 August 1848, and the apparently unpublished notes by J. V. Bridgeman, quoted by Sir Francis Burnand in 'A Genius nearly Forgotten', *Britannia*, London: August, September, November 1907.

[2] *Britannia,* see above.

[3] Walter Lacy: 'Random Recollections', *Routledge's Annual,* London 1879.

[4] Street Guides.

[5] J. C. Hotten: Introduction to G. A. Sala: *Robson,* 1864.

[6] Letter to *The Era,* 6 July 1866.

[7] For a full account of this little theatre, see Malcolm Morley and George Speaight: *Theatre Notebook,* Vol. XVIII, No. 4.

[8] *Punch,* 8 September 1841.

[9] J. A. Cave: *A Jubilee of Dramatic Life and Incident,* ed. Robert Soutar, T. Vernon. ND.

[10] *Ibid.*

[11] F. R. Cooper: *Nothing Extenuate, the Life of Frederick Fox Cooper,* London 1964.

[12] See below.

[13] See (1) above.

[14] William Leman Rede: *The Road to the Stage,* new edition revised and improved, London 1836.

[15] Lou Warwick in *Theatre Unroyal,* Northampton 1974, describes the movements of Jackson's Company for 1842-1843, and these tally more or less with the Bridgeman and Horace Wigan account of Brownbill-Robson's engagements. No mention of him by name occurs in the correspondence which Mr. Warwick unearthed in the Daventry Solicitor's office, but this is not surprising as few playbills survive, and many letters must have been lost. The Company was in Uxbridge in December 1842, and young Brownbill might well have met Jackman there after his marriage in September 1842.

[16] James Douglas: *Theodore Watts Dunton*, London 1904.

[17] Mr. Harry Greatorex, who has made an intensive study of the Nottingham Theatre, has kindly searched the records for me.

[18] Harold Scott: *The Early Doors*, London 1946. The Eagle Tavern, with its Grecian Saloon, was at the corner of the City Road and Shepherdess Walk.

[19] J. E. Ritchie: *About London*, London 1860.

[20] Geoffrey Best: *Mid-Victorian Britain*, London 1971.

[21] *The Era*, April-May 1866.

[22] Francis Burnand: *Britannia* articles: 'A Genius nearly Forgotten', London, August, September, November 1907.

[23] John Hollingshead: 'A Dramatic Meteor'. *Entracte Annual*, London 1898.

[24] *Ibid.*

[25] Burnand quotes information supplied by E. M. Robson, Robson's 'second son' (see Appendix 1 for discussion as to his parentage). E. M. Robson was not born until 1855, so his recollections must have been derived from Mrs. Rosetta Robson, who brought him up and whom he certainly regarded as his mother. During the Grecian engagement she was living with her husband, and it is understandable she should have kept a document such as the 1847 'engagement' with Rouse, which is among the items reproduced in *Britannia* and described as coming from this source:

Grecian Saloon, May 1st 1847.

I, Thomas Rouse, do hereby engage you, Frederick Robson, for one year, on and from Saturday 11th May, to do, fulfil and execute all the duties you have hitherto fulfilled and executed at this establishment, at a salary of Three pounds per week, playhouse pay. To find your own wardrobe, and abide by the rules and regulations of the Grecian Saloon.

As witness my hand this 1st day of May, 1847.

[26] See (23) above.

[27] G. L. M. Strauss: *Reminiscences of an Old Bohemian*, London 1880.

[28] M. Willson Disher: *Victorian Song*, London 1955; and *The Cowells in America*, edited M. Willson Disher, Oxford 1934.

[29] Francis Fleetwood: *Conquest*, London 1953.

[30] William Davidge: *Footlight Flashes*, London 1866.

[31] See also *The Mask*, Vol. 14, No. 3.

[32] Reminiscences of the Old Queen's, *Dublin Evening Mail*, 21 May 1907.

[33] *Observer*, 1 May 1853; *Ibid.*, 10 July 1853.

[34] See (32) *supra*.

[35] R. M. Levey and J. O'Rourke: *Annals of the Theatre Royal, Dublin*, 1880.

[36] J. L. Toole: *Chronicled by Himself*; ed. Joseph Hutton, London 1892.

Part II

Robson of the Olympic

Farren, 1853

1. *The Olympic*

The Olympic, which was to be Robson's home for ten years, was the third theatre of that name on the irregular-shaped site at the corner of Wych Street and Newcastle Street. The second, made famous by Vestris, had been burnt down on Thursday evening, 29 March 1849. The new theatre, quickly rebuilt for under £10,000, was opened on 26 December of the same year.

The architect was F. W. Bushill. Inside, it was an elongated horseshoe, giving good sight-lines from all parts of the house. The stage was 55 feet wide and 45 feet deep, with a proscenium arch of 27 feet high; it had an inclined plane of half an inch to the foot, arranged with working grooves for wings and flats, and there were four traps. Any portion could be removed 'singly' or in combination, so that 'a gulph or chasm' could be represented. The stage machinery was designed by R. J. Strachan. There was a good-sized Green Room, above which were the two 'best' dressing-rooms, and under the back of the pit were four large and two smaller ones. All had water-closets, sinks with running water and fireplaces. There were additional dressing-rooms in the Manager's House in Craven Buildings.

The height from the pit floor to the ceiling was about 36 feet. This ceiling was divided into four compartments decorated by Mr. Aglio to represent the four seasons, and from the centre hung a large chandelier made by Ashley Pellatt. The proscenium arch was a simple frame to the stage in white and gold, decorated in chiaroscuro with representations of the muses, and supporting pilasters with arabesques which incorporated the coats of arms of Lord Craven, the ground landlord, and Mr. Cavell, the proprietor. The upper proscenium boxes displayed masks of tragedy and comedy; the lower, cameos of poets. The gallery and box tiers were divided by gilded and bronzed columns and arabesques, with the usual masks, musical instruments, etc. The Act Drop represented 'An Italian loggia opening upon a Cortile', and was painted by Messrs. Dayes and Gordon, who were responsible for most of the scenery.

The fire had spread to the adjoining property, causing much damage. Some houses were purchased and demolished to give greater space and reduce fire risk. There was now a passage-way, or alley, between the former gallery entrance and the next house in Wych Street. There were two stone staircases to the Gallery, one for entrance and both for exit, and a separate exit for the stalls and boxes. All entrances and exits were fireproofed. 'Several safety measures' were introduced by Mr. J. Palmer, who installed the gas lighting.

Accustomed to think of 'the little Olympic', we might be surprised to learn that its capacity was over 1,700, but this included pit and gallery, into which the audience could be packed to a degree inconceivable in the twentieth century.

Clement Scott praised the Olympic pit for, in addition to the centre seats, there was a raised platform all round the walls, which was a godsend to those glad of the privilege of 'standing only'.[1]

The exterior was unostentatious: an arcade of five arches, three of them entrances and the other two blanks, was surmounted by a series of five windows, and above them a cornice with a low attic. This main frontage was in Wych Street as formerly.

The house was particularly well-ventilated by a large air-shaft over the central chandelier and several other air-shafts or flues, and was serviceable and comfortable by the standards of the day. The safety precautions proved themselves, for the third Olympic never burnt down. It was demolished and re-built in 1889, and in 1905 this fourth theatre was cleared away when the Aldwych and Kingsway were laid out. Its site lies beneath the eastern wing of Bush House.[2]

A popular innovation was the abolition of gratuities to attendants. A free 'bill' was provided for the night's performance, and about 1850 smaller playbills were introduced (approximately 12" x 9"), which developed into the modern folded programme.

The theatre was opened in style on 26 December 1849 by the former lessee, who soon ran into trouble.[3] George Bolton took over for a while, but his management was already moribund when it was decided that he should take the Strand from William Farren, who would move to the Olympic.

The Olympic had had no real run of luck since Vestris left in 1839, and the rebuilding had not ushered in a new era. A less promising neighbourhood for a theatre aiming at more than local patronage could not be imagined. G. A. Sala was to write that in the whole of London there was no dirtier, narrower, more disreputable thoroughfare than Wych Street.[4] The 'rookeries' or courts which surrounded the theatre were some of the worst in London, and were not cleared away until 1862 when George Peabody, the American banker, gave £150,000 to build 'improved dwellings'. Yet Vestris had drawn the town by a well-managed house, good theatrical fare and her own talents. Leigh Hunt said that by pitching her tent midway between city and west end she enticed the sprightly part of the town to see what the city had to offer. The 'sprightly' could come in their carriages, and the middle-classes of the northern and southern suburbs in omnibuses, of which there were 3,000 by 1853.

William Farren, however, had neither the health nor the resilience to revive the great days of Vestris. He needed a star or a really strong policy to entice audiences to Wych Street. He was born in 1787, a contemporary of Macready, son of the Farren who had acted with Garrick. Five years before he took over the Olympic he had a stroke from which he never fully recovered. He and his company transferred from the Strand with no break in their activities but, although he had the best of the bargain, the first season was uphill work.

There were guest performances by Helen Faucit, G. V. Brooke and James William Wallack, and a good resident company including the attractive young comedian, Henry Compton. Farren seems to have favoured drama, such as Buckstone's *Isabelle* and Morris Barnett's *Lilian Gervais,* with the occasional musical play or farce and from time to time a revival of one of his own past successes, *The Vicar of Wakefield* or *The Poor Gentleman.* He was a fine actor of the old school, specialising in old gentlemen — garrulous, genial or eccentric.[5] (He was a great Sir Peter Teazle.)

But this was not enough. Henry Compton's secession to the Haymarket in March 1853 was the final blow. Compton himself was probably seeking not only more money but a better setting for his talents. He was to be replaced by young Robson from Dublin, an unknown quantity. Whether Farren had already seen his promise at the Grecian and sent him to Dublin to further his dramatic education, or whether he had seen him in Dublin, his engagement was something of a gamble.

According to Burnand, the meeting between Farren and Robson took place at the office of a theatrical agent in Bow Street. Robson went straight to the Olympic on his arrival in London, but had not the courage to ask to see the Manager. He was overawed at the thought of shaking hands with one who had acted with Mrs. Siddons, Edmund Kean and Charles Young.[6] It is reasonable to assume that he stayed with his mother, Mrs. Margaret Brownbill, who was still in Lambeth. It was an easy walk from the theatre over Waterloo Bridge with its 1d toll, or there was a horse bus he could take. He was separated, but not entirely estranged, from his wife Rosetta, who was living in Hoxton or Hackney with the children. Young Fred remembered going to visit his paternal grandmother in Lambeth when their father was in Ireland. At some stage after his return from Ireland he acquired a permanent home, south of the river; first in Hercules Buildings, Lambeth, and then at Kennington Green. He took the children away from their mother, and sent them to boarding-schools. But this was not until he was established as 'Robson of the Olympic'.[7]

Meanwhile, he had to justify Farren's faith in him, to learn new parts and meet new colleagues. The chief ladies were Mrs. Stirling, an experienced and polished performer; the 18-year-old Harriet Gordon, who called herself 'Principal Singing Actress' and had a good breeches figure for such parts as Tom Tug in *The Waterman;* Miss Anderton, brought from the Theatre Royal, Manchester, to play the heroine in Morris Barnett's *Lilian Gervais;* Miss Isabel Adams who played the older ladies; Mrs. B. Bartlett who played the really old ladies; and the versatile Mrs. Alfred Phillips.

Mrs. Alfred Phillips was to be more closely associated with Robson than the others, as his Lady Macbeth. She was 30 when Robson joined the Company, and usually played character parts. Besides acting, she wrote six moderately successful plays between the end of October 1851 and the end of September 1853. One of these, a 'Domestic Drama' called *Life in Australia,* first seen on 21 February 1853, was on the popular theme of emigration and gold-prospecting, with a first scene set in Ireland. (Charles Reade's *Gold* had been seen at Drury Lane for the first time on 10 January). She may have had Australian connections, and some Irish blood. In 1855 she was to go to Australia, and appeared in Sydney as 'The Popular Delineator of Irish Character', and 'late principal comedy actress of the Royal Olympic Theatre'. Her husband, Alfred Phillips, also wrote a play for the Olympic: *The Original Bloomers,* making fun of the latest fashion for ladies.

The gentlemen were Messrs. G. Cooke; Kinloch; Laporte; Diddear, Edgar; C. Bender, who had been in the Company when the theatre burnt down, and who now functioned as 'Stage Director', as well as taking small parts; the versatile old stager, W. Shalders, also a scene painter; Hoskins, also Stage Manager; two newcomers, Marston from

Sadlers Wells and Morgan from Birmingham; the two young Farrens, Henry and William; and their father, who appeared in selected parts only. This was not a very strong company on the male side. Compton took his benefit on 16 March, and departed.

Farren had only ten days after Compton's departure in which to prepare the new season, opening on Easter Monday with Morris Barnett's version of Scribe's *Marco Spada*, entitled *Salvatori, or the Bandit's Daughter*, 'with new Scenery, Dresses etc', not to mention a new low comedian. In Holy Week all theatres were closed for dramatic performances and given up to Sacred Concerts, so that Managers and companies were able to concentrate on rehearsal all night if necessary. Farren was challenging the Princess's, which was also producing a version of the same piece, *Marco Spada*, on Easter Monday. As well as the Manager and the actors the stage staff must have been on their mettle: Mr. Shalders was responsible for the scenery; Mr. Matthews, the machinery; Mrs. Lightfoot, the props.; Mr. Allen, Mrs. Rawlings and their assistants, the dresses; and Mr. John Barnard, the music. The little Olympic could not rival the Princess's at this stage, and this was acknowledged by its lower prices: First Price; Boxes 3s; Pit 1s 6d; Gallery 6d; Second Price at nine o'clock; Boxes 2s; Pit 1s. These prices, indeed, nicely indicated the Olympic's status — about midway between Sadlers Wells and the Princess's. Had the evening been a failure, it would have been disappointing to the Company and stage staff, but disastrous for William Farren and Frederick Robson.

2. *'The Country Fair'* and *Macbeth*

Robson did not conquer the Olympic audience on his appearance as Bomba Becatelli in *Salvatori*, the first piece in the bill for Easter Monday, 18 March 1853, although the *Illustrated London News* said he was 'a comedian of intelligence who makes his points with engaging facility'. The 'time of the drama' was thrown back to the age of Innocent X, with setting and costumes 'appropriately brilliant'. The spectacle was worthy of comparison with the Princess's version, with scenery by Lloyd, Dayes and Gordon. Mr. Henry Marston and Miss Anderton had 'capital opportunities for fine, pathetic and serious acting'.

But the house did not warm to the new comedian. 'I don't think much of this young man,' was Farren's comment, according to Harwood Cooper. 'They don't relish him.'

Salvatori was followed by Charles Selby's *Catching an Heiress* with Robson as Tom Twig, the part he had played at the Grecian. Into this he introduced 'The Country Fair', and this turned the tide.

44

Plate 5. Robson in scenes from plays at the Olympic. *Plot and Passion*, 1853 (above) and *Payable on Demand*, 1859.

MR. ROBSON AS MAWWORM IN "THE HYPOCRITE."
PORTRAIT OF MR. ROBSON.

AS SAMSON BURR (Porter's Knot).

AS QUEEN ELEANOR

AS PAWKINS.

Plate 6. Robson in character, as seen by artists. As Mawworm (top left), Samson Burr, Queen Eleanor, and Pawkins.

Plate 7. Robson in character, in photographs. As Shylock, 1853 (top left): Medea, 1856 (top right): Boots at the Swan, 1853 (bottom left); and Daddy Hardacre 1857.

Plate 8. Robson himself. Four portraits.

Farren's comment after 'The Statue Song', as Harwood Cooper called it, was 'That's very good; he's an actor!' An *actor*, not just a comic singer 'with spoken'. He brought to life a variety of characters, each one a finished study. From that moment his place in the Company was secure.

Salvatori and *Catching an Heiress* continued in double harness, except on two occasions when the *Heiress* was replaced by Mrs. Alfred Phillips' *Life in Australia* with Robson as Erasmus Shorthand, 'our own correspondent', played originally by Hoskins. He sang 'Let's be off to the diggings!', and donned female attire to watch a dance of 'natives'. Mrs. Phillips herself played Norah, and both as actress and 'as the avowed authoress' was applauded at the end of the piece when led on by Mr. Farren. The Australian tableaux represented emigrants' tents, the Gold Diggings, a distant view of Melbourne, etc., and were devised by Mr. Shalders. Tents, crushing machines and miners' tools were furnished by Messrs. Deane, Dray and Co., miners' 'dresses' by Mr. Groves of Lambeth Marsh.

Meanwhile, *Marco Spada* was having its own success at the Princess's, with Walter Lacy as Pepinelli (much the same endearing braggart and coward as Becatelli). Lacy and Robson would have liked to see each other's interpretations, but were never free on the right nights.

The Princess's main piece since February had been Charles Kean's spectacular and 'historical' authentic production of *Macbeth*. Robson must surely have seen this on one of his free half-evenings, perhaps running up Drury Lane as far as High Holborn, and then along Oxford Street to the theatre. *Macbeth* was playing to capacity every night, but Walter Lacy would have squeezed him in somewhere.

Young Henry Farren appeared in *Father Mathias*, and then as Quasimodo in *The Hunchback of Notre Dame*, with Robson as Gringoire. This play was quietly dropped after two performances, but one cannot help wondering why Robson was never cast as Quasimodo. He had a good part in an ephemeral comedy by Mrs. Phillips, *Uncle Crotchet*, on 18 April, followed by *Catching an Heiress*. For the first time the 'Song of the Country Fair' was advertised in big black type, and on Wednesday, 20 April, for Mr. Kinloch's Benefit it was given out of context, together with the 'burlesque cachucha' which Robson had performed at the Grecian in 1848. The same night he played Peter Bummel, the comic part in the old melodrama, *The Flying Dutchman, or the Phantom Ship,* but this was apparently no longer to the public taste, and ran for four nights only.

The playbill of 11 April had announced:

Various novelties are in preparation, amongst which not Shakespeare's but Talfourd's 'Macbeth' will be produced with new scenery, dresses and supernatural effects.

The first night was to be 25 April.

Burnand tells us that the Macbeth travestie dated back to Talfourd's Eton days, and that it was first played at 'his Dame's'.[8] A better-known performance was that at the Henley Regatta of 1847, with Talfourd (of Christchurch) as the Lady and Samuel Brandram (of Trinity) as Macbeth.[9]

There was a professional performance at the Strand on 10 January 1848, during the lesseeship of Fox Cooper, Harwood's father. Lady Macbeth was played by Yarnold, well-known for his old men and as a burlesque actor, and Macbeth by Oxberry.

Talfourd was not pleased with this. His criticisms were voiced in a *Theatrical Times* article of 6 May 1848, signed 'Oxoniensis'. He complained that it was

. . . provoking to pun consecutively for an hour to audiences too thin and chilly to force a laugh, to have scenery of any age, time or clime inflicted on one's works, and to find no opportunity given to author or actor.

He would have liked a cockney Duncan, and Paul Bedford as the Lady.

He arranged an amateur performance in his own home, presumably to show how it ought to be done. H. Crabb Robinson remembers going to Talfourd's house to see a drawing-room performance of *Ion*, followed by 'a Macbeth travestie'. 'It got off to some pleasantry' and Brandreth (sic) as Macbeth 'made fun of the character'.[10]

There was one more amateur performance, at the Royalty on Boat Race Night, 1848.

The success of *Macbeth* at the Princess's must have suggested to Farren that a revival of Talfourd's burlesque might be a box office draw, or perhaps Robson first thought of the idea. Anyone who took himself as seriously as did Charles Kean was a sitting-target for parody. Talfourd would have no reason to complain of insufficient attention to scenery and 'putting-on' in the Olympic version.[11]

Farren clearly enjoyed himself at Kean's expense. There is a humorous description attached to each character:

DUNCAN: King of Scotland, a Monarch of large heart but homoeopathic intellects, which is the chief reason of his having 'borne his faculties so meek'.

MACBETH: The original 'Noble Sportsman' who crossed the poor Gypsy's hand with silver, and listened to the stars — his descendants are with us to this day. Etc., etc.

Farren provided a burlesque Introduction, sending up Charles Kean, and his allusions to Pliny and the Icelandic Sagas:
Here is Kean:

The very uncertain information, however, which we possess respecting the dress worn by the inhabitants of Scotland in the 11th century renders any attempt to present the tragedy in the costume of the period a task of very great difficulty . . .
I have borrowed materials from those nations to whom Scotland was continually opposed in war . . . retaining, however, the peculiarity of the striped and chequered garb . . .

Here is Farren:

With respect to the costumes, and the least possible respect to the Authorities (who are singularly vague and unsatisfactory) I have endeavoured to borrow the materials from that Nation with whom the Christian Legislature appears to be constantly at war, but of course without success. Being therefore reluctantly obliged to pay for them, I am anxious they should be as correct as is consistent with propriety and moderate outlay. Pinnock informs us . . . that the early inhabitants of Britain, a few years anterior to this play, were contented with one light overcoat of paint, fitting closely to the figure with the addition of a war club on full-dress occasions . . .
. . . In the time of Severus . . . their garments are represented as of material known as coarse Tweed; I have, however, consulted Berwick on the course of the Tweed, but with no material result; it is however quite clear that of whatever stuff they were composed, their enemies, finding that they had their own work cut-out in subduing the hardy Scots, offered them a peace, and that they eventually made it up between them.

Etc., etc.
The Olympic guyed some of Kean's 'mechanical novelties'. At the Princess's Banquo's ghost appeared within the hollow of a pillar; at the Olympic a skeleton umbrella was produced from a clock-case.

Nigger minstrel tunes provided much of the music: 'Who's dat knocking on de door?'; 'Lucy Neal'; 'Such a gittin' upstairs', etc. Macbeth and the King danced a reel to the tune of Jim Crow, and an 'Apparition of an Ethiopian Serenader' appeared in the second witches' scene. Operatic extracts from *L'Elisir d'Amor, Der Freis-*

chütz and *Les Huguenots* were used, as well as popular songs such as the favourite 'Jeannette and Jeannot'. The book of Talfourd's *Macbeth* does not seem very witty to the reader, and abounds in puns, but it must have come alive on the stage. It is neither the best nor the worst of such hybrid entertainments.

Farren cast Robson as Macbeth, with Mrs. Alfred Phillips as the Lady. Why was this, seeing that Talfourd clearly meant her to be a *travesti* part, and had originally played her himself? Perhaps it was Robson's own choice. Having seen T. C. King and Charles Kean as Macbeth, he may have wanted to emulate them, to express in burlesque the tragic power pent-up in his comedian's body. Visually, this Macbeth was a red-headed Scottish sergeant of militia in a modern uniform, much addicted to whiskey. Did he use a Scots accent, and was the red hair his own? In Samuel Butler's *The Way of All Flesh* Ernest Pontifex describes how Lady Macbeth whips up Macbeth under her arm, and carries him off kicking and screaming. (Mistakenly, he ascribes the part of the Lady to Mrs. Keeley.) Mrs. Alfred Phillips must have been a complete contrast to Robson in physique. Her masterful Lady Macbeth and Robson's small, rather nervous Macbeth must have given a new slant to Talfourd's burlesque.

For ten years Robson had been playing all sorts of low comedy parts to all sorts of audiences with considerable but not overwhelming success. 'Out of this nothing original came'.[12] Farren may have expected no more than competence, and the ability to make the audience laugh with a caricature of Charles Kean's Macbeth. What he had was 'an original creation', the first in a series of portraits unique in nineteenth-century theatre:

The Illustrated London News of 30 April 1853:

> Mr. Robson does not caricature any existing actor, but simply exaggerates the part, painting the terror and horror of the part and the deed in ludicrous colours without altering the outline or feeling . . . A new and wholly original actor . . . capable of giving an air of originality to burlesque itself . . .

The Observer of 1 May 1853:

> His peculiarity is that he really seems to be aware of the tragic foundation which lies at the bottom of the grotesque superstructure; and hence, however extravagant his gestures and articulation, they are odd expressions of a feeling intrinsically serious . . . The Macbeth of *Mr. Robson belongs to no recognised school of burlesque acting*; it is an original creation. (My italics.)

From now onwards there were increasing allusions to this 'tragic foundation beneath the grotesque superstructure', and even suggestions that he should act tragedy in earnest.

For the first week of its run *Macbeth* was followed by *Uncle Crotchet*; later by *Catching an Heiress* with the 'Song of the Country Fair'. On 2 May and during the week *The Miller of Derwentwater* (E. Fitzball) was substituted, in which Robson had the subordinate and undemanding part of Dr. Prussic, possibly because *The Wandering Minstrel* was in preparation.

3. *The Wandering Minstrel, 'Vilikens' and Shylock*

On Monday 23 May, after playing Macbeth, Robson appeared as Jem Bags in *The Wandering Minstrel*. There could not have been a greater contrast. This farce in one act by Henry Mayhew was first performed at the Fitzroy Theatre on 16 January 1834, with Mitchell as Jem Bags, a London 'cadger' and ballad-seller who accompanies his cracked voice on a cracked 'flageolet' (more likely a cracked clarinet), and is mistaken for an eccentric nobleman who has disguised himself as a ballad-singer for a wager. The play became popular. As we have seen, Robson played Jem Bags at the Theatre Royal, Dublin, in rivalry with John Rouse at the Queen's, and sang 'Villikind' (sic) there, possibly for the first time, unless he sang it as an incidental at the Grecian.

Dutton Cook describes the realism of Robson's impersonation:

> So vivid a picture of an outcast street musician, ragged, miry miserable, his limbs racked and distorted with rheumatism, his voice hoarse and broken with constant exposure to rough weather, had not been seen before on the stage. Something the effect owed to a sketch by Seymour . . . but the daring originality of the actor fully manifested itself.[13]

Robson, then, was an innovator in the painfully detailed realism with which he dared to present this disreputable individual. Worse than Jem Bags could be seen round the corner, in the parish of St. Clement Danes, but such figures were not seen in the auditorium. Even the Gallery cost 6d. This was the London of Mayhew, Doré and Dickens, but the Olympic's local audience was recruited from the respectable tradesmen of the neighbourhood, whose names can be read in the street guides, and whose shop-fronts as depicted in contemporary prints belie the bad reputation of the district. Somehow they managed to ignore the Jem Bagses on their doorsteps. Robson himself never lived near the theatre; south of the river was his early home, and later he moved to the north, to Camden Town. But he cannot have failed to meet Jem Bags and his like in Bedfordbury, and as he came to and from the theatre. He must have taken careful mental notes.

Typical of the period is the merriment aroused in the audience by the sight of this pitiable figure:

. . . the exquisite truth by which he imitates the voice, dress, manner and general appearance of his man draws forth shouts of laughter . . .

Thus the *Morning Chronicle* of 21 August. And Francis Burnand records:

What a roar of merriment greeted the appearance of the woe-begone little figure of Robson, who, in smashed hat, shambling on in muddy shoes that could hardly be held together by bits of string finished on the flageolet the last notes of no air in particular, as after looking up beseechingly at the windows of the street, disappointed of coppers, he wandered down to the 'flote' where with an intensely comic look of abject misery, he silently surveyed the already convulsed audience.[14]

There followed 'the very ancient ballad of "Vilikens and his Dinah" ', sung with 'inimitable drollery'. Enthusiastic audiences joined night after night in the Too-roo-ral chorus, and demanded the 'moral' which Robson varied from time to time.

The first edition (Campbell Ransford) was not published until 11 November: 'as sung by Mr. Robson, the symphonies and accompaniment by John Barnard'. The picture on the cover was by Augustus Butler, with a facsimile signature of 'Fred Robson'. This was followed by many other editions (see Appendix) and the song was heard 'everywhere'. It was sung professionally by Sam Cowell and J. L. Toole, and many others less famous.

Between 2 and 27 June the theatre was shut because work on the sewers made it unapproachable, but on 28 June Mr. Farren respectfully informed the Nobility, Gentry and Public that the approach was now complete by way of the Strand and Newcastle Street. He announced a new Drama — *Love and Avarice* — Bridgeman's version of Balzac's *Eugenie Grandet,* for Henry Marston, Henry Farren, Miss Anderton and Mrs. B. Bartlett. Did Robson watch from the wings and plan how he would interpret the old miser? *Daddy Hardacre,* one of his future successes, was another version of the same story.

The last night of *Macbeth* was 2 July, and a new burlesque, *Shylock, or the Merchant of Venice Preserv'd,* by Francis Talfourd was promised for Monday, 4 July. After the first night of this new burlesque the

Observer wrote on 10 July 1853:

> By the assumption of a strong Jewish dialect with the twang and the lisp pushed to the last degree of exaggeration, Mr. Robson made the part eminently grotesque, but he adhered to the principle — exclusively his own — of grounding his eccentricities on a really tragic basis.

The Illustrated London News followed with:

> Mr. Robson's genius is unique . . . His Shylock simply reduces the Jew to a Holywell Street type, and then trusts the rest to the natural development of passion . . . Many of his bursts are truly tragic, and might have done justice to Edmund Kean in his best days . . . Is there after all but a step from the sublime to the ridiculous?

Holywell Street in the mid-nineteenth century was a narrow, dirty lane chiefly inhabited by sellers of old clothes and 'low' (i.e. obscene) publications. It was not far from the Olympic. If you turned down Newcastle Street towards the Strand you would find it on your left. An article in *The Train* commenting on the prosecution of a gentleman living in Holywell Street for selling obscene publications thought the address alone would be enough to convict him. Possibly Robson bought some of his Jem Bags clothes there, and may well have modelled his Shylock on a local character.

Dutton Cook, however, sends him farther afield for his model, describing him as 'a three-hatted Jew from Houndsditch, an old clothesman with snuffling, guttural dialect, vehement of speech and eccentric of action'.[15] The Grecian was not far from Houndsditch, and Robson must have known Whitechapel during his Standard engagement.

There was the same realism in speech, make-up and costume as in Jem Bags. Dirty, cringing, cunning, with his little hands folded on his stomach, his head held on one side, his speech that of Holywell Street or Houndsditch, or a mixture of both, in outer semblance he conscientiously re-created what he had seen and heard. But the man inside was wrought out of his own imagination and his own experience. He may not have suffered racial persecution, but clearly he had known deprivation and insecurity, and his physical disadvantages were always holding him back, keeping him down.

His Shylock had a certain dignity:

> . . . his frenzy might culminate in an odd dance, his grief burst into comic singing, yet . . . he was plainly a child of noble birth.

So much for the sublime, according to one critic. The ridiculous was expressed in his delivery of what another called the 'recondite puns', in the exaggeration of gesture, and in some grotesque dancing. There was a trio polka with Bassanio (Kinloch) and Antonio (G. Cooke) and a crude drunken scene in which Shylock fell into the trough of a practicable pump, declaring he was not drunk to the tune of a song by Henry Russell. 'Young Lochinvar' and 'Tippety Witchet' provided tunes for other songs.

The trial scene proceeded as might have been expected, with puns and scraps of off-Shakespeare such as:

The quality of mercy's not strained
Nor filtered as Thames' water needs to be before it's drinkable.

But a 'Judge and Jury' trial was interpolated:

Scene 5. The Judge and Jury Society, Venice.
How the Chief Baron lights his cigar at nine o'clock precisely.

Mr. C. Bender, as Duke of Venice, was the Lord Chief Baron on this occasion.

Judge and Jury Trials had been initiated by the disreputable Renton Nicholson at the Garrick's Head in 1841, and transferred in 1851 to the Coal Hole in the Strand. He presided over a burlesque court of law, in which counsel at least were usually acted by professionals, but the jury by enthusiastic amateurs. 'Stage business of unquestionable lewdness' was introduced. It is unlikely that Farren would have allowed this in his burlesque, but there may have been some rather risqué gagging, since for the 1859-1860 revival 'the grosser portions of the burlesque' were altered or omitted. For his Benefit Robson secured the services of Renton Nicholson himself, which must have shocked the regular patrons but attracted some who did not usually visit the Olympic.

This is to anticipate. On Monday, 11 July, Farren printed at the top of his playbill:

Crowded houses to witness Mr. Talfourd's burlesque. Mr. Robson's impersonation of Shylock belongs to the histrionic phenomena of the day.

One critic who did not succumb to burlesque Shakespeare, and was reluctant to pronounce on Robson on the strength of his Shylock, was George Henry Lewes:

I object to all these desecrations of fine works, but Shylock had not even a laugh to satisfy criticism . . . The only endurable portion of it was Mr. Robson's performance — which is certainly peculiar, showing mimetic power and significance of gesture, but no humour . . . I must see Mr. Robson in some character not burlesque before venturing an opinion as to his power.[16]

Five years later Crabb Robinson saw Ryder as Shylock in *The Merchant*, and said how much better Robson would have played the part. The 'impersonation' continued nightly, usually followed by *The Wandering Minstrel*, but in the week of 11 July by *The Railway Station*, an old Grecian success.

On Wednesday, 22 July, Mr. Frederick Robinson 'at the suggestion of several friends' performed Alfred Evelyn in Bulwer Lytton's *Money*, supported by the Olympic Company. (Robson had the small part of Stout.) After *Money* Mr. Robinson appeared in four parts in the Musical Entertainment, *Of Age to-morrow*. As if to deflate Mr. Robinson's pretensions, Robson and Mrs. Phillips finished the evening with *A Day after the Fair*, in which he played six parts and she three.

From 8 August *Shylock* was followed by *Boots at the Swan*, another success from Grecian days. Jacob Earwig, the deaf ostler who is always 'getting things wrong', showed another side of Robson's talent in comedy acting, and this was one of the non-burlesque parts in which he was most warmly remembered. Keeley had been the first 'Boots' in 1842. Henry Morley thus compared Robson with him:

> Mr. Keeley was a true Boots. Mr. Robson also is a true Boots . . .
> Mr. Keeley was not only deaf but humorously solid; Mr. Robson, although deaf, is humorously wide-awake. He is the Boots who is brisk and alive to all the humour of the street, who would be preternaturally knowing if he could but hear what people say. In word and look he is more of the *gamin* than the simpleton.[17]

The season of Benefits began in August. Robson took his first at the Olympic, on 15 September; he played Sam Swipes in *Exchange no Robbery*, followed by *Shylock*, including the dubious Judge and Jury show, presided over by Renton Nicholson in person, as already mentioned. Mrs. Alfred Phillips chose a long programme for her Benefit on the following Monday, 19 September: she played Lady Teazle with Farren in his famous interpretation of Sir Peter, given for 'positively the last time', and he seems to have kept his word; Robson was Moses and William Farren the Younger kindly 'gave his services' as Joseph Surface. This was followed by a play of her own, *My Husband's Will*, with Robson as Bonum Longfellow and Mrs. Phillips as herself 'with song'. The evening wound up with *Shylock*.

Thursday, 22 September, was Farren's Benefit and the last night of his management. He appeared in his 'old and favourite part' of Lord

Ogleby in *The Clandestine Marriage;* his 'antiquated, foolish but good-natured old dandy was perfect', and the audience was taken back to the days of the great comedy actors. Mrs. Phillips as Mrs. Heidelberg 'had not been seen before to so great advantage'. In the cast were other Olympic regulars who would not be seen there together again: the eighteen-year-old Harriet Gordon, who had sued Farren for five days' loss of salary while the sewers were being repaired; Miss Isabel Adams, Miss Sarah Lyons and Miss Ellen Pitt; Mr. F. Charles; Mr. G. Cooke (who would, however, return later to the Olympic); Mr. Clifton, Mr. Sanger and the inevitable Mr. Shalders. 'God Save the Queen' was sung by the whole strength of the Company, followed by *Shylock* and *The Wandering Minstrel.*

Mrs. Alfred Phillips went to Australia, where she passed the rest of her life, and the others scattered here and there. Robson and Ellen Turner were the only members of the Company re-engaged by the new Manager, Mr. Alfred Wigan, and even Robson's future was in doubt for a while.

Robson and Farren did not part at once. Together they went to the Theatre Royal, Liverpool, for seven nights, where they played *The Clandestine Marriage, Shylock* and *The Wandering Minstrel.* Farren then retired, and died in 1861.

The debt owed by Robson to Farren in incalculable. It is remarkable that an actor of the old school should have allowed and even encouraged him to develop an original style. Without such backing at this stage in his career he might never have risen above competence and mediocrity. As he was to say in the address written for him by the brothers Brough in 1857:

I could walk when I came here, that's all one,
But here I felt my feet and learnt to run.

And to quote W. Y. Laing's letter in the *Era* of 6 July 1866:

It was only after his return from Dublin that the fire within him thoroughly kindled up.

The encouragement of Farren, the framework provided by the Olympic and its Company, and the response of the audience to his individual style, created Robson of the Olympic.

The Wigans, 1853-1857

4. *Plot and Passion, Windsor and To Oblige Benson*

But Robson of the Olympic had still to win the confidence of Alfred Wigan, the new Manager, who seems to have been doubtful as to the suitability of this new and original actor for his Olympic plans. Wigan knew the house, having acted small parts (Gratiano, Roderigo) there under Watts in 1830, and he had hopes of attracting the fashionable world to Wych Street as in the days of Vestris. Clement Scott called Wigan one of the only gentlemen of the stage, and he was tenacious of his gentility. An admirer of the French school, he modelled himself upon Bouffé, and 'belonged to that epoch of civilisation in which the duty of controlling feelings' was imperative.[18] His acting was unrivalled for finesse and delicate sensibility, but lacked robustness. He was the antithesis of Frederick Robson.

Mr. and Mrs. Wigan were precursors of the Bancrofts and the Robertsons in their ideas of stage management and theatrical discipline, and they also wielded considerable backstairs influence in the fashionable world.[19] Mrs. Wigan was the moving force in the partnership. He 'thought he was acting on his own volition, when in point of fact he was carrying out her wishes . . . a very pushing, sagacious, active, indefatigable woman . . . She was the Lady Macbeth who put daggers into Alfred's hands'.[20] Born Leonora Pincott, the daughter of a showman and grand-daughter on her mother's side of James Wallack, she is said to have been a rope-dancer and performer on stilts in her youth but preferred to forget such youthful activities. Her dramatic talent was small, but she had a certain instinct for the stage, and like her husband prided herself upon gentility. Old Mrs. Winstanley made fun of these pretensions, saying that Mrs. Wigan's sole experience of drawing-rooms had been when, perched upon stilts, she proffered the customary scallop shell for contributions at the first-floor windows of fashionable houses. She certainly helped her husband to acquire 'that more finished style of acting' which was becoming fashionable in the mid fifties.[21] She too had played at the Olympic under Vestris, and must have had ambitions for a revival of the old glories. Her photographs show a hard-faced woman with bright eyes. Alfred looks grave, and undoubtedly gentlemanly. He was also well-educated; his father had been a language teacher, and both Alfred and his brother Horace were good French scholars.

How would Frederick Robson fit in with the ambitions of this genteel and determined couple? The disreputable Jem Bags was hardly the kind of character they planned to present to the fashionable world. And what of the burlesque Macbeth and Shylock? Had not Robson been assisted at his Benefit by the disgraceful Renton Nicholson? An 'Histrionic Phenomenon' he might be, but he was certainly not a gentleman.

Several writers think it was to Mrs. Wigan that he owed his re-engagement. A shrewd business woman, she saw his box office potential, and may have been influenced by his considerable charm. Dutton Cook, on the other hand, says that it was 'the urgent recommendation, almost the entreaty, of William Farren' to which Alfred Wigan yielded.[22] At all events, he was re-engaged.

J. R. Planché wrote for the opening night, 17 October 1853, *The Camp, An Introductory Extravaganza and Dramatic Review*. Mr. and Mrs. Wigan appear on a bare stage and discuss what they shall give their public. One by one the members of the new Company appear, each representing a special line, each with rival claims and suggestions:

Mrs. Chatterley	Tragedy
Mrs. Stirling	Comedy
Miss Corri	Opera
Miss P. Horton	Fancy
Mr. F. Robson	Burlesque
Miss Stevens	Pantomime
Miss Ellen Turner	Hippodrama
Mr. Emery	Spectacle
Signor Galli	Ghost of the old Italian Opera
Mr. Franks	Harlequin
Mr. Harwood Cooper	Clown
Miss Huntley	Columbine

Here then were those who were to be Robson's colleagues.

Mrs. Stirling, then aged 42, was one of the last to exhibit the grand style; her way of taking a curtain call was a lesson in deportment. It seems likely that she gave young Robson some lessons in polished comedy acting. Sam Emery, son of John Emery, was a talented comedian five years older than Robson; Miss Stevens was to be the older lady in various future productions (such as Miss Tite in *Crinoline* and Mother Goose in *The Discreet Princess);* Priscilla Horton, a much-admired Ariel at Covent Garden in 1847, but rather plump by our standards, was already married to T. German Reed, and with her husband later devised and performed the celebrated 'family' entertainments at the Gallery of Illustration; Mr. Franks would be seen in many 'bit parts'.

Harwood Cooper, probably a friend of Robson's from Lambeth days, was a useful actor, who as ostler, man-servant or valet might play an unobtrusive but important part in forwarding the action, without attracting much public attention. From now onwards he was to observe Robson's career at close quarters.

The musical director was T. German Reed, Priscilla Horton's husband; the ladies' costumes were by Mrs. Curl, and the gentlemen's uniforms by Mr. Brown; the scenic artists were Messrs. J. Dayes and J. Wilson. The acting manager was W. S. Emden, who had come from the Princess's, where he had been stage director since 1844.

This elegant 'revue', as the press called it, of the state of the drama was aimed at the fairly sophisticated audience which Wigan hoped to attract. The music included 'La Donna è mobile' from *Rigoletto,* heard for the first time in England in May of that year; an ensemble from *La Sonnambula,* 'Rataplan' from *La Figlia del Reggimento:* the inevitable 'Nigger Song' ('Poor Old Joe' with bones accompaniment); Dr. Arne's bravura aria, 'The Soldier Tir'd'; and the skating music from *Le Prophète.*

There were topical allusions, as this to the forlorn state of English opera:

Mr. Wigan: Have you no new great airs upon your shelves?

Opera: The greatest airs the singers give themselves.

Ballet-on-ice seems foreshadowed:

She tells you, fallen from her high estate
On her last legs she's taken now to skate
Like a bold wench resolv'd at any price
To cut a figure though it's but on ice.

Robson, 'fancifully dressed', bounds upon the stage, and speaks Planché's apologia for burlesque, tracing its literary pedigree 'in his most effective style', and repudiating the suggestion that its aim is but to make people laugh:

Those who think so but understand me half . . .
Did not the thrice-renowned Thomas Thumb
That mighty mite — make mouthing fustian mum?
Is Tilburina's madness void of matter?
Did great Bombastes strike no nonsense flatter?

When Mrs. Chatterley as Tragedy cries:

Unreal mockery hence! I can't abide thee!
he replies:

Because I fling your follies in your face

57

And call back all the false starts of your race
Show up your shows, affect your affectation
And by such homoeopathic aggravation
Would cleanse your bosom of that perilous stuff
Which weighs upon our art — bombast and puff!

This description of the function of burlesque must have pleased Wigan. It claimed high ideals and a literary origin for this sometimes vulgar entertainment.

The Camp was indeed a witty and charming way of introducing the Wigans, their Company and their policy, although *The Observer* thought it too long. Having listened to all the arguments and seen specimens of everyone's art, Mrs. Wigan sums up:

In each of them there's something that is good
Without committing ourselves here to fix 'em
Let's take the best and mix 'em.

But the main piece of the evening was Tom Taylor's *Plot and Passion,* based upon a French original. And here Wigan and Robson clashed in a way vividly described by Harwood Cooper.

Wigan, having cast himself as the romantic hero, Henri de Neuville, and Mrs. Stirling as the beautiful, erring but ultimately repentant Marie de Fontanges, in the pay of Fouché (Sam Emery), cast Robson as Fouché's spy, Desmarets: 'A little elderly man, shabbily dressed, of mean presence, furtive of movement, fawning of manner, cunning and treacherous', not really 'within the range of a comic actor'. The part exploited his physical drawbacks, without giving him any scope for his comic talents.

According to Harwood Cooper (himself cast as Griboulle, who brings an important message in Act II), Robson 'went grumbling all over the theatre, and told his manager that he had no right to make him play a First Old Man's part, since he was engaged for low comedy'.

Wigan's reply brings the scene to life:

I flatter myself I have discrimination in the casting of my people for the characters. I am positive you are the very man for the part. You appear as my low comedian in the burlesque introduction, which identifies you as my low comedian. Don't get ventilating your supposed grievances to everybody in the theatre!

Mr. and Mrs. Wigan were disciplinarians, and they knew at the Princess's and Drury Lane there was a rule which forbade any person being engaged for a specific line of business exclusively, and the penalty for refusing a character was dismissal. 'My people', as Wigan grandly called his Company, must treat him with as much respect as if he were Macready or Charles Kean.

Was he sincere in his claim that his new low comedian was 'the very man' for Desmarets? Or did he think the part so unimportant that it would put Robson in his place?

Robson's grumblings were understandable. At first reading, Desmarets seems a poor part, totally lacking in humour, and considerably overdrawn. He is a sinister presence, moving silently, knowing everyone's secrets, and uttering the occasional 'great' speech; such as this, addressed to Marie:

> I am not young, not pleasant to look at; I have no graces of speech; I am what the world calls a spy and an informer . . . but I have a will like iron, and a head which under any other circumstances might have made a different man of me . . .
> You spurned me once in a way which few men of a less determined spirit would provoke or endure twice. Yet I provoke it again, for proud as you are I love you still.

Etc., etc.

This was not the Robson the Olympic knew, although perhaps the germ of Desmarets may be seen in the unpleasant Wormwood in *The Lottery Ticket*.

Robson submitted to discipline, played the part and acted everyone else off the stage, including his manager and Mrs. Stirling. In some ways it was the greatest success of his career, and caused many to predict for him a future that was never realised.

Henry Morley wrote:

> The drama had been but a short while opened on Monday night when the general interest fixed itself on that ill-dressed dwarfish figure, and whoever else might occupy the scene, the eye still sought him out.[23]

The Observer, having praised the ensemble, paid this particular tribute to Robson:

> The most remarkable feature was, however, the acting of Mr. Robson . . . his wily servility, his malicious chuckle, his placidly treacherous face are wonderfully truthful . . . it is felt that that peculiar talent which infused something of tragedy into burlesque has here for the first time found legitimate employment.

In 1882 Dutton Cook still vividly recollected the evening:

Acting so intense, so passionate, so pathetic was new to the audience. The actor roused the house to an extraordinary display of enthusiasm. A success so striking had not been known since the days of Edmund Kean. His method might be crude, over-spasmodic, verging on extravagance, but surely there was something of Kean's power and impetuosity, his rapidity of utterance, his significance of gesture and alertness of action, something even in his tones of voice, tender and musical in the upper register, hoarse and grating in the lower . . .[24]

Because this type of acting was new to the audience at this time, people were tempted to compare it with that of Edmund Kean. It was the other side of the coin from the realism of Jem Bags, and equally original in the eyes of his contemporaries. How would a modern audience react to Robson's Desmarets or for that matter to Kean's Richard III? With laughter, with embarrassment, or with hypnotised surrender?

Mrs. Stirling threw all her pathos into Marie, and apparently bore Robson no ill-will for outshining her. Wigan was not without jealousy, according to Harwood Cooper, a jealousy which came to a head just before the Windsor Theatricals scandal (see below). Yet Mrs. Stirling and Wigan were given the final curtain, when the repentant Marie falls upon Henri's neck, and tells the audience that her storm-tossed bark will now seek wedded life's calm bay, ending with the tag, spoken centre:

The master passion Love — that still is Lord of all.

(The play was originally billed as *The Master Passion*.)

The play attracted large audiences, and the emergence of the 'new' actor was a topic of conversation and debate. Was he a low comedian, with an outstanding gift for burlesque, or was he potentially a great tragic actor?

The news of his success reached Charles Dickens in Genoa, whence he wrote to his wife on 29 October:

I am pleased to hear of Mr. Robson's success in a serious part, as I hope he will now be a fine actor.[25]

By 'a fine actor' Dickens probably meant something in the line of his friend Macready. If he had watched Robson's career since the days when he sang comic songs in 'low' haunts, this development must have been particularly interesting to him.

George Henry Lewes, having resolved to see Robson in a non-burlesque part, went to see *Plot and Passion* and wrote thus:

Plate 9. Frederick Robson as a young man.

Plate 10. Robson as Jem Bags, 1853.

. . . He is a remarkable, a very remarkable actor; and I shall be much surprised if he do not become, in his way, a great actor; for he has the two essentials, originality and mimetic power. Humour he has none; and it is not as a low comedian he will take rank, but as an actor of Bouffé parts, in which character is represented by truthful details . . . those critics who credit him with tragic power make a fundamental mistake . . . he seems to me unequal to the force, breadth and impassioned dignity of a tragic scene. It is not passion so much as excitability he portrays . . . details taken separately were admirable; but they made no homogeneous creation.[26]

Lewes's distinction between excitability and passion in Robson's acting is particularly interesting. In the same article he made the further criticism that Robson never represented emotions in their *subsidence,* for his transitions were too rapid. But, with his mobile face and his intelligence, this was something he could remedy, Lewes thought. Robson, as we know, was to exploit the rapidity of these transitions, rather than seek to cure them. What Lewes considered a weakness became admired and even imitated as 'Robsonian'.

Robson was never to have another part like Desmarets, but he was to use some of the same effects: the 'wild cry of anguish' became the 'shriek' in *Daddy Hardacre* which Henry James never forgot. For 'effects' we might substitute 'tricks', were it not that writers such as John Oxenford and Cecil Armstrong expressly denied that Robson achieved his results by 'tricks'. Those who thought he would be best known by his rapid successions from tragedy to comedy were proved right, but whether this was a quality or a limitation is arguable. His physique was against him for pure tragedy, although it was an asset in Desmarets and the Yellow Dwarf, and no drawback in Daddy Hardacre. Kean was considered short at five foot six and three-quarter inches; Robson was barely five foot, with a large head, and small feet and hands.

But in the autumn of 1853 it seemed to most people that he had no limitations, that there need be no bounds to his ambition. 'The little man was undoubtedly the big fact at the Olympic', as Henry Morley wrote.[27]

The Camp and *Plot and Passion* continued to draw, and on 28 November there was a three-week revival of *The Wandering Minstrel.* E. L. Blanchard described Robson as 'great in Vilikens', and he took notes of the 'moral' and spoken interludes to provide the publisher Davidson with a version near to that actually performed. Blanchard did not know Robson, but heard at the Wrekin that he was about thirty-six and in weak health.[28] (He was 31.)

On Thursday, 26 January 1854, 'Mr. Alfred Wigan, Mr. F. Robson, Mr. Vincent, Mr. White and Mr. H. Cooper' had the honour of appearing at Windsor Castle, where Charles Kean organised the theatrical entertainments for Her Majesty. The plays were *Tender Precautions* (T. J. Serle) and *The Bengal Tiger* (C. Dance). In the former the Olympic Company was joined by that of the Princess's, and the chief parts played by two distinguished stage couples, Mr. and Mrs. Keeley and Mr. and Mrs. Wigan. In the latter, Robson played the character part of David, an old family servant, who helps a pair of young lovers to gain the approval and the fortune of Sir Paul Pagoda, a rich nabob (Alfred Wigan), frustrating the matrimonial intentions of Miss Yellowleaf (Mrs. Wigan).

Alfred Wigan prized these Windsor 'Commands', although the financial rewards were not great. Charles Kean estimated the losses he incurred in managing these entertainments as £1,689 over a period of six years. Macready's accounts of visits to Windsor were less than enthusiastic, although he admired the Vandycks. However, when *The Bengal Tiger* was given at the Olympic on 27 and 28 January, Wigan had the satisfaction of saying it was 'as performed before the Queen and HRH the Prince Consort at Windsor Castle'. The system of payment and the complications it involved will be explained when we come to the Windsor Theatricals scandal.

On 2 February the Olympic audience was introduced to Robson's Wormwood in *The Lottery Ticket,* always one of his most successful 'disagreeable parts'. It was played with *The Bengal Tiger* and *The First Night* (in which there was no part for Robson) until H. F. Chorley's *The Love Lock* brought novelty on 13 February, with Robson as Peter Handelbaum. But after three performances it disappeared for good.

Tom Taylor's 'new comedietta', *To Oblige Benson,* on 6 March proved a permanent addition to Robson's repertoire. It was on the popular theme of marital boredom, and Robson, as Mr. Trotter Southdown, a gently absurd and essentially bourgeois character, had to portray both real and feigned jealousy. H. Crabb Robinson admired the way in which he distinguished between them.[29] There were moments even in this mild comedy when he showed he had the capacity for a serious part, but the role belongs to the group of bewildered, not-too-young gentlemen in which he seemed to invite the audience to laugh with him at some farcical predicament. Such roles were a long way from the grotesque realism of Jem Bags, the melodrama of Desmarets or the uneasy fantasy of his great extravaganza parts, but equally characteristic. His success as Mr. Trotter Southdown was lasting and of a kind Mr. and Mrs. Wigan could approve. He was supported by Sam Emery as Benson, Mrs. Stirling as Mrs. Trotter Southdown, and Miss Wyndham ('magnificently buxom', according to Marston) as Mrs. Benson.

For the first fortnight *To Oblige Benson* was teamed with *The Bengal Tiger* and *The First Night,* but on 20 March, as if to show that Robson was not his only new attraction, Wigan replaced *The Bengal Tiger* with *The Wrong Box,* in which Robson had no part, with new scenery and dresses; music by T. German Reed; a good singing part for Mrs. Reed; parts for Miss Wyndham and Miss Ellen Turner, and for Mr. Frederick Robinson of the Lyceum. (It may be remembered that he had taken the theatre at his own expense on 29 July of the previous year). It was said of him that 'for parts in which the gentlemanly element prevailed he had all the conditions', which must have commended him to Alfred Wigan. But neither his gentlemanly bearing, nor the new music, scenery and dresses, could ensure the success of *The Wrong Box.*

On 21 March when Queen Victoria visited the Olympic she saw *To Oblige Benson* and *The First Night* (one of Wigan's personal successes), and on 28 March she was given a triple Robson bill: *Plot and Passion, The Wandering Minstrel* and *The Lottery Ticket,* three contrasting roles and not one of them gentlemanly. He was already established as a great favourite with Her Majesty, and she visited the Olympic five times that season to see him. The books of all the plays she saw were prettily bound in white paper sprinkled with gold stars. On the flyleaf is the date and V.R. in her own hand.[30]

On Easter Monday another Grecian success was revived — *The Happiest Day of My Life* (J. B. Buckstone) — in which Robson played the harassed bridegroom, Mr. Gilman, supported by Mrs. German Reed, Miss Marston, Mrs. Chatterley and Messrs. White, Franks and Rivers. Queen Victoria saw it on 4 July.

Plot and Passion, The Wandering Minstrel and *The Lottery Ticket* ran until the end of May in different combinations, so that half-price patrons could see them all. It was beginning to be the fashion to 'go and see Robson', and to see him more than once in the same part. Those were the days when 'all London' was discussing the brilliant little genius, and Clement Scott was glad to avail himself of half-price in the pit at nine o'clock to see Robson in one of his great parts.[31]

Horace Wigan, Alfred's younger brother, joined the Company that season from the Theatre Royal, Dublin. He was a good foil to Robson, 'a quiet, solid undemonstrative actor', according to Joseph Knight who knew him personally.[32] Rowley in *The School for Scandal* was the perfect part for him. J. Kenney's feeble burletta *Fighting by Proxy* first brought him in the same bill as Robson in the 1853-1854 season, but this 1833 piece was dropped after nine performances.

Another 1833 revival, however — W. B. Bernard's *The Mummy* – surprisingly ran for about a month. J. Reeve had been the first Toby Tramp at the Adelphi, and many provincial comedians had followed him. Robson as Toby puts on calico bandages and pretends to be a mummy, in order that Captain Canter may impress his intended father-in-law, an antique collector. In the course of the proceedings Robson introduced Ford's 'The Lost Child', which he had sung as an 'Incidental' at the Grecian, and which would have been more suitable in a Music Hall, though doubtless he was very funny in this cockney scena about a mother from the 'rookeries' of Holborn who loses her child and finds him again. Miss Marston, Harwood Cooper and Horace Wigan were his colleagues.

But revivals were not enough. Wigan thought that the theatre needed novelty, and wrote to an unknown correspondent (Tom Taylor?):

> Have you anything that might suit me? — something not dependent upon scenic effects nor great numbers.[33]

(in other words, something cheap to mount).

Whether or not this appeal was answered, it was the revival of yet another 1833 burletta, Charles Dance's *Hush Money,* which brought crowded houses to see Robson on 4 June. Jasper Touchwood suffers remorse because he fears he has caused his deserted sweetheart to drown herself, and believes that Tom Tiller, the waterman, suspects him of having pushed her in. Robson represented Jasper's mental agony, and his subsequent relief when he finds he is not guilty, with 'wonderful artistic detail'. 'Robson's acting wonderful, but piece bad', was Blanchard's summing-up. Liston had been the first Jasper, and Robson's comic acting was sometimes compared with Liston's. Partly Liston, partly Kean, thought one observer, but in truth he was neither — he was just Robson.

When a novelty appeared at last it was J. Palgrave Simpson's *Heads or Tails,* in which Robson had a part certainly not good enough for him, but in which he elicited roars of laughter, chiefly by pretending to have a bad cold; his continual snuffling was considered 'extremely natural'. Feeble as this farce was, it stayed the course for some weeks, and was succeeded by another, equally feeble — *Perfect Confidence* by an unknown author — with Robson as Mr. Easy. 'The absurdity of the situation enabled Mr. Robson to come out with his usual force', and 'he gave every shade of the character and elevated the incidents to their most advantageous position', was the best the press could say. It was successful enough to be honoured by Princess May of Teck and suite, and 'a full and fashionable audience', and to be played for Wigan's Benefit on 12 July.

On 11 August, the last night, Wigan gave 'an amusing congratulatory address', speaking of the contradictory advice given him when he took over the Olympic, and the prognostications of failure. He had gone his own way, and 'thanks to an indulgent public, a working, willing Company, and an impartial and considerate press' he had achieved success in the first year.

On Saturday, 12 August, there was the usual Benefit for W. S. Emden, Acting Manager, consisting of *To Oblige Benson, The First Night* and a miscellaneous concert, with contributions from Louisa Pyne, Monsieur et Madame Weiss, Rebecca Isaacs, and . . . Mr. Robson with 'The Song of the Country Fair'.

The Wigans had certainly done well. A Command Performance at Windsor, five visits by Her Majesty and one by Princess May of Teck had set the seal of Royal Approval on their endeavours to rehabilitate the Olympic. They had built up a good ensemble of players, who had made the most of rather thin material. But it was undoubtedly Frederick Robson who had done most for the Olympic.

Yet he had been given nothing original, nothing to stretch his powers, since Desmarets. The impression is that the Wigans, or at least Alfred, were keeping him in what they considered his rightful place, as a resourceful comedian with an endearing personality, and a great box office attraction, whatever the rubbish he appeared in. Robson may have been contented enough. His successes were easy. It was not hard to make people laugh. There was little sign during the Wigans' first year of the darker side of his gifts, and of the agony it would bring him. He was on the way up, and so far the way was smooth.

Gradually 'you began to hear at clubs and in critics' coteries — at the Albion, and the Garrick, and the Café de l'Europe, at Evans' and Kilbeck's, the Reunion in Maiden Lane, and at Rules Oyster Room — rumours of a new actor'.[34] A letter from Charles Kemble, dated September 1854, invited him to dinner at 8, Albany Terrace, New Road, 'on Saturday next at ¼ before 6 o'clock'. Such an invitation from the brother of Mrs. Siddons to the recently-arrived comedian was indeed an honour.[35]

As for his private life, it seems that he was living in Hercules Buildings, and made there a home for his two children. According to her Declaration, he visited his wife, Rosetta, on an average three times a month, and the result of one of these visits was the birth of Edwin May on 12 January 1855 (see Appendix: *The Paternity of E. M. Robson*).

From 14 until 26 August Robson was engaged at the Queen's, Dublin, where his acting

. . . produced a perfect furore . . . the theatre positively overflowing.

He played Desmarets, Shylock, Jem Bags and Jacob Earwig, and was engaged for four more nights, with a Benefit on Saturday, 2 September.

5. *A Blighted Being and The Yellow Dwarf*

The theatre re-opened on 9 October 1854. Improvements had been made in the ventilation, the Circle enlarged and re-seated, and a row of upper box stalls constructed which might be retained for the whole evening (Second Price 2s.). The German Reeds had left the Company. Mr. Barnard was still leader of the Band.

The first week brought nothing new, but on 16 October Tom Taylor's *A Blighted Being* (from the French *Une Existence Décolorée*) gave Robson more scope than for some time. Job Wort is a disappointed literary gentleman who wishes to commit suicide painlessly, and makes a bargain with an Irish chemist, O'Rafferty (Horace Wigan), to supply him with the means. Having swallowed what he believes to be poison, he begins to enjoy life and even to fall in love. His 'agony of apprehension was realised with such minute accuracy that it rose to the height of the tragic'. E. L. Blanchard wrote on 17 October: 'See Robson in wonderful performance of Job Wort'. The plot was so slight as scarcely to fill-out its 44 minutes' playing time, but Job Wort remained one of Robson's *tours de force*.

The two Robson successes, *Perfect Confidence* and *A Blighted Being,* continued with the addition of a revival of *The Lottery Ticket.* Charles Dance's 1833 *Beulah Spa* opened the evening on 13 November with good parts for nearly everyone. The beautiful Julia St. George made her début in Wigan's Company that night in Madame Vestris' old part, singing 'By the margin of Zurich's fair waters' and 'Why seek to hide the deep emotion?'. She had played opposite Robson in Dublin, and was to dispay her fine figure and good singing voice in many future successes. Robson was Magnus Templeton, the overgrown schoolboy who thinks he is in love with his mother's maid.

On 11 December Jem Bags showed his disreputable person for the first time that season, and 'Vilikens' was sung every night in the pre-Christmas period to the continued delight of audiences.

Meanwhile the extravaganza for Boxing Day 1854 was in preparation: J. R. Planché's *The Yellow Dwarf*. Both J. R. Planché and Tom Taylor must have watched Robson's development with interest since the first night of the Wigan régime when he had served each of them so well, in *The Camp* and *Plot and Passion* respectively. Tom Taylor had already given him some congenial parts, but it was Planché's Yellow Dwarf which was to be memorable.

Planché wrote that when he became interested in adapting *Le Nain Jaune* from Madame d'Aulnoye's *Contes de Fées* he thought he saw in Mr. Robson such a representative of the yellow dwarf as he might never see again. He was not mistaken:

. . . So powerful was his personation of the cunning, the malignity, the passion and despair of the monster, that he elevated Extravaganza into Tragedy. His delivery of the lines slightly parodied from Othello over the dead body of Desdemona moved Thackeray, 'albeit unused to the melting mood', almost to tears. 'This is not a burlesque', he exclaimed, 'it is an idyl.'[36]

If not quite an idyll, it was certainly not a burlesque. The author's own sub-title, A Fairy Extravaganza, best describes it. The 'book', although written in rhymed couplets, is nearer in style to Gilbert-without-Sullivan than to the Talfourd *Macbeth* or *Shylock*. The songs are set to well-known airs, many of them operatic.

Gam-Bogie, the Yellow Dwarf, saves the Queen (Mrs. Fitzalan) from savage lions on condition that she promises him the hand of her daughter, Princess Allfair (Miss E. Ormonde). To an air from *Der Freischütz* he admonishes her:

But your promise keep with me
And your daughter Queen will be
    Of this fine Empire — O!
Here I sing and feast and sport,
Dancing though my legs are short,
    As in *Lanky*shire — O!

There follows 'a Lancashire clog hornpipe', specially introduced for Robson, 'who made a popular feature of it in the provinces'. It will be remembered that Dan Leno was a champion clog-dancer in his early years. Planché considered both song and dance best omitted, but arranged as a polka they became a popular number. Harwood Cooper tells us that years later Queen Victoria used to hum it in private, and commissioned 'the equerry Sir Spencer Ponsonby' to get a copy for the Royal Christmas celebrations. As one of the surviving members of the original cast, Cooper was able to trace it.

Returning to the story: Princess Allfair wishes to marry not the Yellow Dwarf, but Meliodorus, King of the Goldmines (Julia St. George). After various transformations and fairy adventures, the

Dwarf stabs Meliodorus with a magic sword, which Allfair seizes and kills herself. It was the dwarf's lamentation over her lifeless body that so moved Thackeray.

The dead lovers are turned into palm trees, as in the original story, but Syrena the Mermaid (Miss Bromley) changes them back to their own forms:

A tale of mirth to close at such a season
On two dull trees would be the dullest treason.

To the tune of 'The Old Folks at Home', the happy couple sing

Let other miners seek the diggins'
Far, far away
Here on this minor stage of Wigan's
I'm more inclined to stay.

The Yellow Dwarf casts off his villainy, and sings the 'moral' to the tune of 'Vilikens':

Now all you young folks who are home for the holidays
And children of all growths who hate melancholy days
Come add to the number of Allfairs adorers
And join every night in the popular chorus
Too roo ral . . .

Drawings of Robson as Gam-Bogie sometimes verge on caricature, as does the statuette illustrated in Planché's works and on the cover of the sheet music. But the small oil painting in the Enthoven Collection in the British Theatre Museum brings the character to life in a remarkable way. Here we have the 'monstrous orange-tawny head', and the 'flaps of ears projecting forward like those of a dog' (G. A. Sala), the 'demon dwarf of one's imagination, made-up like one of Fuseli's elves' (*Observer*). The eyes seem blue and piercing, possibly an effect of make-up; in the early portrait in the possession of Mrs. José Smith they are light brown.

The make-up caused domestic friction, according to Harwood Cooper:

Cooper, since I've been playing the Yellow Dwarf I have dyed all our sheets yellow. The old woman's in a towering passion this morning in consequence . . .

This was presumably the powder make-up usual in the nineteenth century, but very skilfully used. Harwood Cooper tells us that as Masaniello (1857) Robson painted with 'what is called grease-paint, not known at that time among professionals'.

The Old Woman in question may have been Rosetta, about to give birth to Edwin May (later known as E. M. Robson), or Mrs. Sarah Manly, who claimed to be Mrs. Robson in the 1861 Census (see below), or some other lady temporarily sharing his bed and board. Harwood Cooper writes that Robson had 'no moral control . . . victim to a woman's attractions', but whether he meant one particular woman or women in general is not clear.

G. A. Sala describes Gam-Bogie as the

> jaundiced embodiment of the spirit of oriental evil: crafty, malevolent, greedy . . . insatiate . . . you laughed and yet you shuddered. He spoke in mere doggerel and slang. He danced the Lancashire clog hornpipe, he rattled out puns and conundrums. Yet did he manage to infuse . . . an unmistakably tragic element. The mountebank becomes inspired.[37]

The grotesque bordered on the terrible, and it was not uncommon for an audience to become hysterical.

Gam-Bogie comes from a world different from that inhabited by Mr. Trotter Southdown, Jacob Earwig and the rest, from that of the burlesque Macbeth or Shylock, or the verminous Jem Bags. Yet in each characterisation was the same attention to detail of make-up, costume, gesture and movement, the same identification with the character, whether trivial, grotesque or terrible. As Westland Marston said, 'He had the gift of gifts, self-identification'.[38]

This 'Christmas Piece' ran for exactly five months, played nightly in a triple bill with various short farces or 'petites comédies', in at least one of which Robson would appear, changing his style of acting as he changed his make-up.

There was Mr. Sowerby in Francis Talfourd and Alfred Wigan's *Tit-for-Tat* — a ridiculous character, thrown into a fit of jealousy in the first act, portrayed with deadly seriousness, and revenging himself upon his tormentors in the second. His fellow-husband was Sam Emery. Alfred Wigan as a younger man, not married until the second act, had an opportunity to show the polish of his acting. It was an ensemble piece, notable for two reasons: it showed what the Wigan method could achieve, and that Robson did not always hold the centre of the stage. Together with Emery, Wigan and the ladies Bromley, Maskell and Turner, he was one of a good team. Queen Victoria saw it on 6 March, and again on 7 May, the last week of its run. The bill of course included *The Yellow Dwarf*, which she is said to have commanded no less than five times. No Easter piece was needed in 1855.

Charles Dance's 1832 *Kill or Cure* gave Robson another lightweight part as Brown, a landlord troubled with a bad temper and a scolding wife (Mrs. Wigan). The first night was 15 April.

Saturday, 26 May, was the one hundred and twenty-second and last performance of *The Yellow Dwarf*, and to mark the occasion Alfred Wigan presented a silver cigar case to Robson, inscribed:

To

Frederick Robson

as a token of

PERSONAL REGARD

from

ALFRED WIGAN

Presented on the 26th of May 1855

The 122nd night of

THE YELLOW DWARF

They had evidently sunk their differences for the time being. In face of such a great piece of acting (and such a Box Office success) Wigan stifled any remaining jealousy. The cigar case is still treasured by the family of Robson's descendants.

There were no sensational new parts for Robson during the remainder of the season. Old favourites were revived, such as Planché's 1839 *Garrick Fever,* in which he played Decimus Gingle and burlesqued Garrick, and *Poor Pillicoddy* (J. M. Morton), his first appearance in the part of the nurseryman at the Olympic. Married to the widow of a man lost at sea, his happiness is ludicrously marred by dreams in which his predecessor has been rescued and returns to claim the lady.

On Friday, 22 June, Alfred Wigan's Benefit was preceded by a riot, in protest at his having enlarged the stalls at the expense of the pit:

The Universal feeling of disapprobation found energetic expression. Up started an indignant paterfamilias, and in a loud and decided tone demanded 'Where's the pit?'.

This cry was taken up by all the affronted pittites, about fifty of whom climbed over the new line of demarcation, and quietly took their places in seats which they considered their rightful territory.

This brought Mr. Wigan out, and he was received 'with a hurricane of disapprobation, which lasted for some minutes'. He expressed regret, but said he had given due notice of the curtailment, which had been carried out in other theatres.

'Never to anything like such an extent!', was the reply. The two policemen did nothing, and Mr. Wigan said he must leave the matter to the good feeling of the audience. The seats which had been taken by assault were retained.

The School for Scandal then commenced, and the performance soon settled down. Mr. Wigan's plausible Joseph was one of his best parts, but some of his hypocritical remarks gave the pittites a further excuse to express their indignation. Mrs. Stirling as Lady Teazle 'looked superbly' in the costume of the period, Mrs. Wigan as Mrs. Candour 'very handsome', and the 'little part of Moses was one of those finished artistic sketches which show the talent of Mr. Robson' and demonstrate how 'an actor of genius can make a great part of a short one, and throw much variety into a small space'.

Mrs. Wigan chose *The School* for her Benefit also, and it was played off and on that season, teamed with *The Bengal Tiger, Plot and Passion, Perfect Confidence* or *Still Waters*. For his own Benefit Robson offered *The Yellow Dwarf, Plot and Passion* and 'The Song of the Country Fair', and for Emery's he appeared not only as Moses, but as Jacques Strop, the comic villain in Selby's *Robert Macaire*.

The bill for the last night of the season was *Perfect Confidence, Still Waters* and *The Wandering Minstrel*, so Jem Bags and his 'Vilikens' had the last word.

On 6 August 1855 the Company began a short season at Sadlers Wells, giving *Tit for Tat, The First Night, The Wandering Minstrel, To Oblige Benson, The Yellow Dwarf* and *A Blighted Being*, together with 'The Song of the Country Fair'.

The Observer forecast on 5 August:

> Mr. Robson is no stranger to the northern districts of the metropolis, and we have no doubt that a numerous throng of admirers, who in days gone by have laughed at his drolleries, will avail themselves of the opportunity . . .

and Harwood Cooper noted:

> Wigan takes Sadlers Wells, thinking the local Grecian favourite would attract.

But admirers from the northern districts showed little enthusiasm for their former favourite, and the usual Olympic audience did not patronise the Islington season, in spite of improved transport and reduced prices. There may have been some snobbery both direct and indirect in this lack of support. The season from 6 to 18 August was not a financial success.

On the Monday, 20 August, Robson was back in Dublin, at the Queen's, where his welcome left nothing to be desired. The theatre was crammed and many were unable to obtain admission. He played *The Yellow Dwarf, Boots at the Swan, To Oblige Benson, The Wandering Minstrel, Catching an Heiress* and *Plot and Passion*. Both 'Vilikens' and 'The Song of the Country Fair' were specifically mentioned by the press. According to *The Era*, 'Vilikens went tremendously', and was usually encored three times. So many were disappointed on 1 September, his Benefit night, that the engagement was prolonged by three extra nights.

On 9 September he was at the Theatre Royal, Birmingham, with *The Yellow Dwarf, To Oblige Benson, A Blighted Being* (having been acted by him before the Queen on four occasions 'by express command'), *Tit for Tat, The Lottery Ticket* ('as performed before Her Majesty and the Court'), and 'The Song of the Country Fair', by particular desire. His Benefit was on Friday, 14 September, and the last night Saturday, 15.

Once more he crossed the Irish Channel, and on Thursday was back in Dublin for another six nights' engagement.

6. *The Discreet Princess and Medea*

The Olympic had been entirely re-decorated by Mr. Warne of Soho Square, and re-opened on Saturday, 20 October, with *The School for Scandal,* followed by 'an amphibious piece of extravaganza' by Sterling Coyne, *Catching a Mermaid,* 'never acted'. This was apparently produced for Robson to sing 'The Song of the Country Fair' in a new context, as the manager of a country fair. Perhaps the new context disconcerted him, since Harwood Cooper says: 'First night of Catching a Mermaid. After his song, "Statue Fair", memory failed him, went to the finish'. The lapse does not seem to have been noticed by the press.

The press praised the setting, and also Robson's execution of the song and the concluding dance, 'in which his agility was put to the test but he succeeded admirably'. *The Era* said of Titus Tuffin that the immense effect produced arose not from over-colouring of any description, but 'from a just and true representation of the real thing'. Miss Bromley, Miss Stephens, Mr. Clifton, Mr. White and Harwood Cooper were also in the cast. *Catching a Mermaid* was a success and was played nearly every night until Christmas, with *The School, Plot and Passion* and *Still Waters* as the serious offerings. On the lighter side, a new Robson farce, *Five Pounds Reward,* was added to the old favourites.

This was an English version of the French *Une Montre Perdue*

(Marc Michel and Martin). Mr. Benjamin Boslethwaite leaves his watch at the house of an old flame in circumstances entirely innocent, but fears that when the watch is returned his wife will think the worst. The press considered the defects of this piece to be obvious, but the thin humour was kept up to the end by the force of Robson's unrivalled energy and his display of nervous excitement. A kind of manic vitality seems to have kept Robson going in the thinner farces, as if he dared not relax for a moment lest he and the audience discover what rubbish was being enacted.

In the 1855 Box of Olympic Playbills in the British Theatre Museum (Enthoven Collection) is a prompt copy of this play marked 'Return to Mr. Robson'. It was bought for 2d by Guy Little outside Dobell's shop and sent to Mrs. Enthoven on 14 March 1942.

Meanwhile, he and the rest of the Company must have been busy with the preparation of something more worthy of his talents: *The Discreet Princess,* Planché's Christmas extravaganza.

During the pre-Christmas period Ford Madox Brown visited the Olympic, and saw on 12 December *Catching a Mermaid, Still Waters* and *Five Pounds Reward.* He thought the English theatricals went 'dooced slow' and the whole place felt 'headachy'. He admitted that Robson was 'tremendous' but 'getting spoiled'.[39]

There was nothing slow or headachy about the Boxing Day extravaganza *The Discreet Princess or The Three Glass Distaffs,* and no need for Robson to push himself into a frenzy to hide the feebleness of his material. Planché sub-titled his piece 'A New and Doubly Moral Melodramatic Fairy Extravaganza', founded on the story of *L'Adroite Princesse.* 'Doubly Moral' alluded to some features introduced from *Mother Goose and the Three Golden Eggs.*

The King goes to war: his three daughters are shut up in a tower, each supplied with a glass distaff which will shatter at the slightest indiscretion. Idlefonsa (Miss Marston) is idle and always falling asleep. Babillarda (Fanny Ternan) never stops talking, but Finetta (Julia St. George) is as wise as she is beautiful. Their retreat is discovered by the wicked Prince Richcraft (Robson). His wiles cause the distaffs of the two elder sisters to break, but Finetta vanquishes him, and after various vicissitudes she marries the noble Prince Belavoir (Miss Maskell).

There are topical allusions to the Crimean War, including King Gander's excuse that he was 'coming home on urgent private business', a phrase rather too often used by officers asking for home leave. Lord Clyde in the audience took this in good part.

The music, arranged by Mr. Barnard, included airs from *Il Trovatore* and *Le Domino Noir,* 'Bartelmy Fair', 'Like the lightning', a polka by

Allary, and 'The Ratcatcher's Daughter'. 'Di Quella Pira' from *Il Trovatore* had words set to it which seem to anticipate *The Mikado*:

> Let him appear, oh
>   Shan't he get toco*
> For yam as surely
>   As surely as I stand here

Messrs. Gray and H. Gray were responsible for the scenery; 'appointments and decorations' were made by Mr. Lightfoot; Mr. Sutherland was the machinist; the costumes were by Mr. Dommett and Mrs. Curl.

In Prince Richcraft Planché had written a part as worthy of Robson as was the Yellow Dwarf. G. A. Sala thought Robson's impersonation the best he had ever done, though he did not think much of the piece:

> In Richcraft you see the unceasing longing to be revenged on nature for her ill-treatment; the life-long rage at his deformity . . . The deformity pervades everywhere, without its being insisted on. It is scarcely apparent in his dress; but the heart is hunched, the soul squints . . .

Again:

> In the midst of your convulsions of laughter at his most excellent fooling — there will suddenly come upon you a feeling sharp and thrilling as a galvanic shock, and very nearly akin to terror . . . Is the man laughing at you, and himself and all the world? Is he showing you a parti-coloured soul as well as a parti-coloured body? . . .[40]

Henry James described Richcraft as he appeared to a small boy:

> I still see Robson slide across the stage in one sidelong wriggle, as the small, sinister Prince Richcraft of the Fairy Tale; everything he did at once very dreadful and very droll, thoroughly true and yet none the less macabre, the great point of it all its parody of Charles Kean in 'The Corsican Brothers' . . . [41]

(Incidentally, Wigan had played Chateau-Renaud, the villain, with Charles Kean as Louis dei Franchi, in *The Corsican Brothers* at the Princess's in 1852.)

Richcraft, like Gam-Bogie, gave Robson the opportunity to incarnate all that was evil and morally twisted, in contrast with the rather endearing qualities of the bewildered gentlemen who sat for many of his stage portraits. But it was essential to a Planché extravaganza that

---

*Toco=a schoolboy punishment

evil should be not merely conquered but reformed at the fall of the curtain, and that the children should not go home frightened. Robson came back to his good-humoured self in the trio finale.

Finetta sings (to the tune of 'The Ratcatcher's Daughter'):

At Christmas time what'er the rhyme
    It should convey a moral.
For giving you a piece with two
    With us you will not quarrel.

Babillarda adds:

The Yellow Dwarf to Easter ran
    And a very long time arter
And our Princess may do no less
    If you'll but kindly start her.

The reformed Prince Richcraft ends up with:

Wych Street's not far from Westminster
    As you come up from the Strand O!
And here we are at Temple Bar
    With the City close at hand O!
There are buses vot run to Islington,
    And t'other side of the water;*
So we trust you'll bring ev'ry mother's son
    With his purty little father's daughter.

The Discreet Princess ran until the end of April, not quite as long as *The Yellow Dwarf*. On 12 February Queen Victoria and the Prince Consort went to see it, for the first time. They saw it again four times before the end of the season.

E. L. Blanchard was there the same night, but either did not stay till the end, or was too distracted by the Royal visit to concentrate, since it was on 2 April he wrote:

. . . saw at night first time Robson all through in Discreet Princess; wonderful and painfully intense performance.[42]

Alfred Wigan was away indisposed in January, a warning of the more serious illness which was to cause his temporary retirement the following year, but on 12 May, while Robson was on leave, he appeared in *Retribution* (Tom Taylor), with the beautiful Miss Herbert, Miss Marston, and Messrs. George Vining, Murray and Leslie. This was a sensational piece, having nothing but wickedness to com-

*There had been a north-south route since 1837.

mend it, thought *The Illustrated London News*. *The Spectator* of 2 August admitted that it was the most popular play of the summer, just as the shocking *Traviata* was the most popular opera. It was violence, not sex, which made *Retribution* wicked. Yet Queen Victoria honoured Wigan with a visit to see this shocking piece on 26 May, during Robson's absence.

On Thursday, 29 May, there were official rejoicings to mark the conclusion of the Treaty of Paris and the end of the Crimean War. This was the first 'Peace Illumination' since the introduction of gas-lighting, and those who remembered the streets lit by a tallow candle in each window pane for the rejoicings of 1814 and 1815 were dazzled. So that the crowds might have a good opportunity of seeing these splendours, theatre managers cancelled evening performances and substituted 'morning performances' at two or three o'clock in the afternoon.

Robson was back that day for a morning performance of *Catching a Mermaid* and *The Wandering Minstrel* from 3 o'clock until 5.30. The two subsequent nights he played in *The Wandering Minstrel* only, then after two nights off, two more nights in *The Wandering Minstrel*, but on Monday, 9 June, he was himself again as Adolphus Fitzmortimer in *A Fascinating Individual*, a farce written for him by the Olympic actor, H. Danvers. Mr. Walton (Sam Emery) wants Adolphus for a son-in-law, but Adolphus is already pledged to a widow, and employs ingenious stratagems to blacken his own character and put Mr. Walton off. Clever and laughable as Robson's performance was, it put too much weight upon a very weak play, thought *The Observer*. Yet the audience laughed heartily, and Robson (called before the curtain) 'gave the piece out for repetition'. This nonsense ran for four weeks, usually in a triple bill with *Retribution* and *Catching a Mermaid*.

A Conjugal Lesson, adapted by Mr. Danvers from the French of Messieurs Delacour and Miraud, brought Robson and Mrs. Stirling together in a duodrama. Mrs. Lullaby finds what she considers incriminating evidence in the coat pocket of her husband the morning after he has spent an evening of brandy and cigars at 'The Frolicsome Oysters'. It transpires that he has taken Brown's coat by mistake, and moreover that Brown has been luring him from home so that he himself may make improper advances to Mrs. Lullaby. Robson gave his 'jealousy act', which 'bordered sometimes on the frantic', and Mrs. Stirling gave a polished performance of a young matron, born to govern 'by coaxing or command'.

Robson's next part was in Robert Brough's burlesque of Ristori's *Medea*. Adelaide Ristori was thirty-four, the same age as Robson, when she came to the Lyceum with her *Medea*. It is right to speak of

Plate 11. Robson as the Yellow Dwarf, 1854.

Plate 12. Robson as Timur, 1860.

'her *Medea*', since the version was third-hand Euripides: Legouvé's French adaptation translated into Italian by G. Montanelli. Rachel had refused the part, and Ristori accepted only on condition that the murder of the children should take place 'off'.

She first played the part in Paris at the Salle Ventadour on 4 April 1856, and on 6 June it was seen at the Lyceum with an Italian company. All theatregoing London flocked to see her. A photograph of her in the part eight years later shows a regal figure and a rather masculine face. Her greatest asset was probably her beautiful voice.

The Ristori sensation was a boon to burlesque writers. Brough must have worked fast, probably with Robson's co-operation. J. C. Hotten says that there was a 'freemasonry of genius' between these two gifted men. Brough was clearly inspired by Robson, and his capacity for curdling the blood, half in jest, half in earnest.

Medea had nothing of the idyll or the fairy play about it. It was an avowed burlesque of the Legouvé play, and parodied not only Ristori's performance but the conventions of a whole school of acting. But the final result, first seen on 14 July 1856, was something more than a burlesque, because of Robson's tragic gifts. Jane Stedman says that 'the tragic scope of Robson's Dame was unique, depending as it did upon the temperament of an unusual actor rather than on the playwright's lines'.[43] Robson, indeed, did not specialise in 'dame' parts. Macready considered it not difficult to act like Ristori; it was just a case of 'a melodramatic abandonment or lashing-up to a certain point of excitement'.[44] Such a lashing-up was one of Robson's gifts. As a result, there were times when, in spite of the puns, he came near to taking the part seriously.

Dickens, who was not impressed by Ristori, wrote to Macready:

> Being in Town last Saturday I went to see Robson in a burlesque of *Medea*. It is an odd but perfectly true testimony to the extraordinary power of his performance . . . that it points to the badness of . . . 's acting in a singular way by bringing out what she might do and does not.
>
> The scene with Jason is perfectly terrific; and the manner in which the comic rage and jealousy does not pitch itself over the floor of the stalls is in striking contrast to the manner in which the tragic rage and jealousy does. He has a frantic song and dagger dance, about 10 minutes long altogether, which has more passion in it than . . . could express in 50 years.[45]

Perhaps the scene of the children's murder and its aftermath epitomises the ambiguity of Robson's acting style:

77

MEDEA is seen standing alone on steps, c., quivering with emotion — a reeking knife in her hand — the Children lying on the steps. (Apparently dead.) Jason stops horrified, seeing the bodies of his children.
JASON: My boys both murder'd! Who has slain them?
MEDEA: You!

The stage directions admonish the actors to carry the whole action 'as in tragedy'. But at the spine-chilling 'You!' Medea looks down at the dagger in her hand, and finds that it has turned into a jester's bauble with cap and bells. Bewildered, she asks:

Who's been employing magic and cajolery
To change my serious business to tomfoolery?

Medea becomes Robson again, steps out of the almost real tragedy, and sings a comic finale with the other characters to bring down the curtain.

This was to be Robson's fate: the dagger would turn into a jester's bauble, and his great tragic scenes end in humorous anticlimax.

There are many accounts of the effect produced on the audience. *The Observer* of 27 July gives a general impression:

In some parts he displayed much power, in others much comic humour, and occasionally true pathos . . . The imitated passage of the panther bounding on his prey — a cat leaping upon a rat — was given by Robson with great earnestness. The stealthy, sliding motion of the cat, her silent watching of her prey, and her final fierce leap to catch and kill . . .

Before the curtain rose on the first night, Dr. Strauss and the author went behind, where they found Robson in a state of extreme nervousness because he had been told Ristori would be in the house.[46] Dresser, call-boy and prompter tried in vain to bring him to his senses:
'Now, Mr. Robson, you're on, Sir!'
Robson grasped the two children by the hand, unable to remember his lines, and gasped in an hysterical whisper: 'The word! The word!' One of the children, Rosina Ranoe, came to his rescue with

My Grecian friends, with deep humiliation
I stand in this disgraceful situation.

Before she had finished the couplet, Robson had pulled himself together, and made his entry. Rosina Ranoe married Francis Burnand some years later, and herself made a good career in burlesque. She recalled that she and the other 'child' were given presents of money, and she was given a doll as well, in recognition of her special services. He never again forgot those entrance lines.[47] But:

This Medea of Robson's! What strength it took out of him!

His intensity varied from night to night during the run of the piece. (Burnand again)

This nervousness was to intensify with time and with success. Success, indeed, made him the more nervous, lest he should not be able to keep it up. 'I must not fail in a part!' he told Harwood Cooper.

Medea ran till the end of the season (13 September). Planché's 'petite comédie', *The Green-eyed Monster,* was given for Robson's Benefit on 16 July, and played off and on for some weeks with *Medea* and sometimes *A Conjugal Lesson,* or a piece like *Delicate Ground* in which Robson did not appear. Blanchard saw him on 9 September when he

Dined at home, and then went to the theatre, merely to see Robson, and that I did to my perfect satisfaction. His variety of power is beyond all my expectations. I could not at first recognise him in the florid, smooth-faced Baron. The green-eyed monster, jealousy, is admirably represented by him. Afterwards, I saw him in the parody of 'Medea'. A gentleman who sat near me in the pit told me that his burlesque imitation of Ristori was excellent.[48]

On 15 September he began a fortnight's season at his old home, the Queen's Theatre, Dublin. *Medea* was the chief attraction, supported by Mrs. Webb as Orpheus and Miss Simpson as Jason. The writer in *The Freeman's Journal* of 16 September spoke of

. . . the passionate display of histrionic power that well-nigh appalled by its terrible earnestness and desperation.

There was more in a similar vein, very different from this same journal's opinion on 9 January 1852 that his speciality was 'this peculiar walk of broad comedy'.

He showed other facets of his art in *To Oblige Benson, Boots at the Swan, A Fascinating Individual* and *The Wandering Minstrel,* with 'Vilikens and his Dinah'.

The engagement was prolonged another fortnight to include *The Yellow Dwarf, The Lottery Ticket* and *Hush Money.* Of the last *The Freeman's Journal* wrote with more enthusiasm than literary style:

Such of the audience as have witnessed the acting of Mr. Robson in the Medea travestie may well be surprised at the versatility of his genius on seeing him personate a character so opposite in a dramatic view.

For his Benefit and 'positively last appearance' on Saturday, 11 October, he appeared in 'the celebrated Comedy of *Law and Lions*' (D. W. Jerrold) as Jemmy Mammoth.

Monday, 13 October, was to have been his first night at the Theatre Royal, Manchester, but he was 'indisposed' and did not appear until Wednesday, 15. In the four days at Manchester he appeared as Desmarets, Medea and Jasper Touchwood *(Hush Money)*. *The Era* considered the spy Desmarets to be a creation peculiar to Robson, with its occasional displays of 'extraordinary earnestness' and its 'comicalities'. His make-up as Medea forcibly reminded the spectators of Ristori. Saturday was his last night.

7. *James Rogers and the Windsor Theatricals Row*

The Olympic opened for the 1856-1857 season on 13 October without Robson. He had apparently not entirely recovered from the Manchester indisposition, and he was not back until 27 October in *Tit for Tat* and *To Oblige Benson*. *The Observer* said the theatre was as usual 'fashionably attended' to welcome him on his return.

James Rogers made his first appearance that same night as Mr. Easy Boulter in *Tit for Tat*. *The Observer* thought his get-up as a London swell admirable, but the rest of his performance 'defective'. Wigan and Robson played admirably together, Wigan's quiet and finished style being an admirable foil to Robson's excitability.

'Jimmy' Rogers had been making a name at the Strand, particularly in travestie burlesque parts. He had a certain physical likeness to Robson, enough for Harwood Cooper to describe him as his 'double or fetch'. Harwood Cooper ascribes his engagement to Wigan's jealousy of Robson's popularity, and suggests there was a plan to get rid of Robson by introducing this rival low comedian. Success may have gone to Robson's head, making him difficult to keep in what Wigan considered his place, and his indispositions must have given rise to anxiety for the future. Whatever his reasons, Wigan was to regret the engagement of James Rogers.

This gentleman appeared with Robson on 24 November in *Jones the Avenger,* Talfourd's version of *Le Massacre d'un Innocent* by Messieurs Varin and Michel, as Shrilly Piper, and received a pat on the back from *The Times*. Robson as Jones, a young painter, is bound by oath to avenge the death of an uncle and kill an unknown gentleman of the name of Tomlinson. Tomlinson (G. Cooke) goes through the whole piece unaware of the plot against him. Jones exhibits a terrifying thirst for slaughter and, when he (wrongly) believes the deed done, is paralysed by remorse. *Jones* ran until the week before Christmas.

On 18 December R. B. Brough's *Crinoline* was introduced, chiefly, it seems, to give James Rogers a good 'drag' part as Nancy Bitters. Robson was cast as Mr. Coobiddy, which he considered an inferior part.

'You would call this a Walking Gent, wouldn't you, Cooper?', Robson said to Harwood Cooper. 'Wigan, I can see, wants me to throw up my engagement. I'll play it!'

Harwood Cooper comments on the 'luck' which attended Robson's refusal to be provoked. Rogers was sacked within two months, Wigan became ill, and Robson was to find himself not only undisputed first comedian but also part-lessee and manager of the Olympic. This is to anticipate the events of early 1857.

On Boxing Day 1856 Planché's *Young and Handsome,* based on *Jeune et Belle* of the Comtesse de Murat, was presented. The English adapter indulged 'his constant desire to elevate the character of extravaganza'. The piece was very well-received, but lacked the originality of *The Yellow Dwarf* or *The Discreet Princess.* The recently-recruited Miss Swanborough was Princess Young and Handsome, who (like Strephon in *Iolanthe*) was only half a fairy; Miss C. St. Casse made her first Olympic appearance as Cupid; James Rogers had the small but important part of Jealousy ('not quite in his line, but his appearance was picturesque, and he played it carefully and like an artist').

As Zephyr, Robson had a star part to make up for his down-grading in *Crinoline,* but it was feeble stuff after Gam-Bogie, Prince Richcraft and Medea. His great scene was a 'pas de fascination', tripping round the stage, occasionally stepping on a flower or a leaf, and dancing on it à la Taglioni:

> The critics all own I
> First taught Taglioni
> To dance on a sun-flower or peony . . . *

The music, arranged by Mr. Barnard, included extracts from *La Sonnambula* and from 'that very naughty *Traviata'; '*Comin' through the Rye'; and 'that very popular Yankee song, "Bobbin' Around" '. Mrs. Wigan was in charge of the whole production. Topical allusions included one to the failure of the British Bank, which had suggested to Dickens the Merdle crash in *Little Dorrit.*

(*In allusion to the famous ballet 'Flore et Zephyre', caricatured by Thackeray).

There were Command Performances at Windsor on 15, 22 and 28 January. Preparations for the first of these had begun in October 1856, and by early January the cast for *The School for Scandal* was settled; the strong Olympic contingent included Mr. and Mrs. Wigan as Joseph Surface and Mrs. Candour; George Vining as Charles; Robson as Moses; and Leslie as Careless. Other theatres provided Benjamin Webster as Sir Peter; Mrs. A. Mellon (formerly Miss Woolgar) as Lady Teazle; Leigh Murray as Trip; etc.

To understand the subsequent vexations, it is necessary to give a brief account of the system of payment at Windsor. Sometimes a complete production would be transferred from a particular London theatre. Sometimes a production would use actors drawn from several theatres. When so many actors were required from one theatre that the manager had to close, he was paid a lump sum, plus 'double salaries' or 'extra salaries' for those appearing at Windsor. It was understood that each actor should receive double salary for the Windsor night, or seven nights' salary instead of six at the end of the week. When performers were singly engaged, they were paid according to scale: £10, £5, £3 (and 10/- for supers).[49]

On the night of 15 January Wigan had closed the Olympic without informing Charles Kean in writing, although the fact was mentioned in the press. He should have received £80 for the closure, and enough to pay his actors a double salary for the Windsor night, instead of which Robson and the Wigans had been paid £10 each, Vining £5 and Leslie £3, and there was no payment for closing the theatre. This misunderstanding was eventually cleared-up, not without some bad feeling. Colonel Charles Phipps, Private Secretary to the Prince Consort, mediated between Kean and Wigan. Finally, Wigan received the £80 cheque, and the actors were allowed to keep their scale payments — surely generous treatment. There was clearly a leak to the press, which prepared the way for the much worse 'scandal' which was to follow.

The performance on 22 January involved two Olympic performers only, and passed without incident. On 28 January, however, *Hush Money* was given with an all-Olympic cast: Robson (the lead); Mesdames Marston, Stevens and Wigan; Messrs. Addison, Cooke, Danvers, Murray and Rogers. Wigan notified Kean of his intention to close the Olympic; he received £80, and also the extra to enable him to pay the nine actors a double salary for the Windsor evening.

Perhaps this had not been properly explained to James Rogers. On the Monday following *Hush Money* (2 February) he 'waited upon' Mr. Elliott, Magistrate at the Lambeth Police Court, and handed to His Worship the following note:

Sir — Allow me to present to the poor-box the enclosed 13s. 4d., being the amount received for performing at Windsor Castle on Wednesday evening last.

The same morning there appeared in the *Morning Chronicle* a paragraph alleging that those who had appeared at Windsor on 28 January were dissatisfied with their remuneration.

On 9 February the *Morning Chronicle* raked up the old grievance that Wigan had not received £80 for closing the theatre, etc., a grievance which had been amicably and even generously settled, and added the story of Mr. Rogers and the 13s. 4d. *The Times* repeated all this and came out with a thinly-veiled attack on Kean.

The next night, 10 February, Rogers appeared as Nancy Bitters in *Crinoline* and, when asked by 'her' mistress how much money was due to 'her', replied: 'Give me my thirteen and fourpence and let me go!', which understandably 'set the whole house in a roar'.

Worse was to come. On 11 February Robson appeared as Titus Fulgent in *A Splendid Investment,* 'a new and original farce' by W. Bayle Barnard. Having invested £1,000 on the prospect of a certain gentleman being married to a certain lady, Titus is involved in various absurd situations which gave Robson the opportunity to display many comic devices, including one of his rages. This was followed by *Young and Handsome,* in which he sprained his ankle during the *pas de fascination,* but carried on until the end. The next day he went to the theatre in a cab, the ankle being black and blue. He wished to play in the farce, but Wigan would not let him. A doctor's certificate to the effect that Robson could not appear was displayed, and caused consternation among playgoers. *Crinoline* was hastily substituted for *A Splendid Investment,* and James Rogers was put in Robson's place as Zephyr. The next week Rogers appeared in Robson's part in the farce also.

If Wigan had ever planned to replace Robson with Rogers permanently he could no longer contemplate it. Although Rogers had apologised both for the gag in *Crinoline* and for the Poor Box incident, he could hardly be *persona grata* at Court, and Court patronage meant so much to Wigan. *Young and Handsome* was taken off on 24 February, and on 26 February Robson came back as Titus Fulgent and as Mr. Lullaby in *A Conjugal Lesson* with Miss Swanborough as Mrs. Lullaby, Mrs. Stirling's old part. The dust began to settle. James Rogers' name soon disappeared from the Olympic roster. (There was no personal animosity between the two comedians, it seems, for Robson appeared for Rogers' Benefit in March 1858.) Colonel Phipps and

Wigan suffered from the incident in their respective ways: Phipps found it difficult to enter into all the 'sensitive sensibilities' of the profession, and Wigan feared that his having unavoidably 'promoted' James Rogers might have caused offence at Windsor. But the worst sufferer was Charles Kean, who resigned his post.

After his return Robson's first part was that of Mr. Brown in *Thieves, thieves!* (Anon). Driven by burglars to take refuge in a chimney, Mr. Lushington emerges covered with soot, a dénouement which brought the curtain down to much applause, but, in spite of Robson, ably assisted by Mr. Vining, *The Era* reckoned the piece 'a decided failure', seldom to be witnessed within the walls of the Olympic.

But at last Robson was to have a part worthy of him — *Daddy Hardacre* – which had its first night on 25 March.

8. *Daddy Hardacre*

Messieurs Bayard and Duport's dramatic version of Balzac's *Eugenie Grandet* had been seen at the St. James's in 1842, with Bouffé as the miser. J. V. Bridgeman's English version was played at the Olympic during 1853.

F. Palgrave Simpson's English adaptation must have been written for Robson. Of all his non-burlesque parts it is the one which gave fullest scope to his special gifts, and is so well-documented that we can get near to what 'seeing Robson' for ourselves must have been like.

The following account is based on those given by various authors, particularly John Oxenford's article in *The Times,* and Henry Morley's *Our Recent Actors,* Chapter XIV.

To a greater extent than in any other character Robson showed in *Daddy Hardacre* 'the man turned inside out'. He had clearly devoted close thought to re-creating the outward aspect of the miser: his way of moving, his clothes, his speech, 'the dialect of a south-eastern county', his lined face, his turned-down mouth, his unkempt hair. Various minor details lingered in Henry Morley's memory for years: his chuckle at his own astuteness, his care of the furniture and the clean tablecloth, the tone in which he expressed his resentment at having to give hospitality: 'How ugly yon fellow looks with his mouth full!'.

Avarice worked in his veins and in his sinews. The preternatural shrewdness which he exercised both in getting and in keeping was so diffused over his whole nature that the most trifling act was under its influence.

Two stimulating causes were at work: ravenous cupidity, and a consciousness of superior shrewdness. Both could be disguised as concern for his daughter's welfare. His love for this daughter was almost childish yet, even while she knelt before him and he caressed her, he remembered that she was wearing her dress out at the knees.

How Robson built up this character could not be described; it had not merely to be seen, but to be watched carefully through the first act. In the second, the ruling passion possessed him like a demon.

The Times criticised the piece at this point for 'making the explosion too intense in its duration', but praised the untiring force and energy with which Robson supported 'the long continuance of passionate despair', as he knelt howling over the site of his lost treasure, and crawled on all fours up from the cellar. This would have been fatal to an inferior actor. *The Illustrated London News* spoke of 'the minute touches' and 'broad unmistakable strokes' as he groped over the spot, and crawled upstairs in the climax of his agony.

Henry James' recollection of this scene fifty years later presents us with a problem. He describes

> . . . the prodigious effect of Robson's appalled descent from an upper floor, his literal and headlong tumble and rattle of dismay down a steep staircase occupying the centre of the stage, on his discovery of the rifling of the chest.[50]

How are we to reconcile this headlong tumble *down* with crawling *up?* The scene specifies 'Stairs from below with stage open' and 'Staircase with platform off'. The stage directions say that Hardacre is to go downstairs to 'the vault', where his treasure is kept, and come up again, half-suffocated with his loss.

Did Robson change the action after the first night in order to make the more terrifying effect, moving the hiding-place of the treasure to the upstairs landing? This would also mean a change in interpretation: as depicted by the first-night critics Hardacre was so broken as to be incapable of violent movement such as Henry James describes:

> . . . his impetus hurled him, a prostrate scrap of despair (he was a tiny figure, yet so 'held the stage' that in his company you could see nobody else) halfway across the room.

Or did Henry James confuse his memories of Daddy Hardacre with some other Robson part? The prostrate scrap of despair might have been Gam-Bogie or Prince Richcraft.

Rage and a wild frenzy followed the discovery that his own daughter was the culprit. Daddy Hardacre seized a chair meaning to throw it at her, but dropped it. The 'swelling waves of passion' gave way to 'the still waters of despair', then to a softening of his feelings and the final reconciliation. After the dénouement, he rushed to the footlights and invited the whole pit to come and see him 'at his own house'. The old servant hinted at the expense, but the miser (with a luxurious chuckle) reminded him that the guests must pay at the door.

This final transition from deadly earnest to joking with the audience must surely have come as a shock, acceptable though such an ending might have been in a burlesque. The ease with which Robson discarded his tragic persona is disconcerting.

As for vocal expression, though Robson's voice was perhaps the weakest part of his dramatic equipment, yet as Hardacre he 'coloured' it to express each transition: his 'changed, almost choked' voice after the discovery; the exhausted voice in which he threatened to have the thief 'hanged — hanged — hanged!', expressing a depth of hatred from which the listeners recoiled; and the repeated 'shriek of alarm' which Henry James could not forget — all these changes were at his command.

What of the rest of the cast? *The Times* considered it would be wrong for any of the other characters to have 'violent utterances of feeling', with the exception of the daughter, who had an opportunity to express 'intense, enduring affection'. Miss Hughes (her first appearance at the Olympic) played the part 'in a most natural and unaffected manner . . . without once attempting to make herself too prominent'. The other parts were 'efficiently played' by Mrs. Stephens, and Messrs. G. Vining, G. Cooke and H. Leslie. But without the support of this well-drilled Olympic company Robson could not have made his 'points', and achieved what his contemporaries considered a masterpiece.

F. Palgrave Simpson must be given some credit for writing a part so suited to Robson. He did not have an easy time with the Examiner of Plays, George Alexander Redford. There was no objection morally, but 'O Lord!' had to be omitted, and 'O God!' altered to 'O Heavens!'.[51]

Harwood Cooper has an enigmatic note:
'Waistcoat for Daddy Hardacre. Dresser Lygo and Newport market.'
Clearly he meant to expand this. Presumably it means that Lygo went to Newport Market, Leicester Square, to buy the fancy waistcoat which can be seen in the pictures of Daddy Hardacre.

9. *Edinburgh; Masaniello; Wigan's illness and retirement*

As was customary, the Olympic was shut the week before Easter, but there was no such practice in Edinburgh, and Robson played there for six nights, 6 to 11 April inclusive.

The Daily Scotsman produced a leader the morning after his first appearance in *Hush Money* and *Medea,* which contains some of the most perceptive writing on Robson's style of acting:

> Mr. Robson is not a star — he is a meteor. His acting is of a most peculiar order . . . belonging to the class Polonius indicated in the epithet 'Tragical-comical' . . . Intensity is in a certain sense his chief characteristic . . . intensity in burlesque, seriousness in shamming . . Thalia grinning through the stern lips and hollow eyes of Melpomene.

On the opening of *Hush Money:*

> The moment the firm, short little figure walks over the stage . . . Robson's gestures and expressions of cold and impatience in this little solitary opening scene reminded us of nothing so much as of Macready in 'Hamlet' waiting for the expected ghost . . .

On *Medea:*

> He is as weird and terrible as the witches in Macbeth, and as grotesque and vulgar as Mrs. Gamp, while his transitions are so sudden from one phase of character to another that he absolutely seems both tragic and comic, serious and shamming, furious and in fun, all at one and the same instant.

During the week he played — besides *Daddy Hardacre* — *Lottery Ticket, Conjugal Lesson, Catching an Heiress, Blighted Being* and *Shylock.*

Among the supporting cast were Kate Saville and the young Henry Irving. According to Austin Brereton, Irving played 428 parts in Edinburgh.[52] Among those he might have played with Robson are: Adolphus Jobling in *The Lottery Ticket,* Captain Killingly or Captain Poodle in *Catching an Heiress.* Many years later he said to Seymour Hicks about Robson: 'Yes, Robson — er — Robson — a good actor, but not great — yes, yes, he was great. He was great enough to know he could only be great for three minutes'.[53]

Robson was back at the Olympic on Easter Monday for *Daddy Hardacre* and *Thieves, thieves!,* a taxing evening's work. *Daddy Hardacre* was such a success that on 27 April the Free List was suspended, with all complimentary admissions, except for the press. On 4 May a revival of *Young and Handsome,* in which he played Zephyr, was added to *Daddy Hardacre.* Another extravaganza was promised as an afterpiece. Clearly his ankle had quite recovered.

He appeared with Mrs. Stirling in a condensed version of Murphy's *All in the Wrong*. Crabb Robinson, whose hearing was not as good as it had been, took a seat in the stalls, 'in order to enjoy Robson to perfection'. He found him good in the Murphy, but not superior to Mrs. Stirling, and the piece was dated. Then he saw *Daddy Hardacre:* 'the rage and despair were incomparable'. He enjoyed his evening very much, and walked back late to Russell Square.[54]

The promised extravaganza — *Masaniello*, 'a Fish Tale in One Act' by Robert B. Brough — was brought out on 2 July, with Robson in the title role. The printed copy was dedicated to Mrs. Wigan. The author thanked her for her admirable stage management and numerous happy suggestions, including the excellent idea of 'adding to the piscatorial aberrations of Masaniello in the mad scene' some reminiscences of Robson's past successes.

The piscatorial aberrations are found in 'I'm a shrimp' (to the tune of 'I'm afloat'):

I'm a shrimp, I'm a shrimp of diminutive size
Inspect my antennae and look at my eyes . . .
I'm a shrimp, I'm a shrimp to be eaten with tea

H. Barton Baker describes how Robson reduced his body to boneless limpness.[55] The mad scene includes:

My Lord, the Earl of Hammersmith is taken.
Stop! That's in Hamlet'. I'm Masaniello.
To be or not to be — that's in 'Othello'.
Translated into Irish for Ristori
Pop goes the Weasel, that's from 'Trovatore'!

He breaks off into a portion of the dagger dance from *Macbeth,* and then part of *The Yellow Dwarf* hornpipe.

The press thought that

Masaniello himself, a fishmonger on a small scale, is just such a person as the genius of Mr. Robson delights to embody . . . the odd and impressive mixture of the quaintness of low comedy with true passion and pathos . . .

There was also praise for the mounting of the piece, and for Miss Swanborough's 'graceful and refined Alphonso', and nine lines devoted to G. Cooke's 'Policeman 7 of B. Division', and his parody of 'The Death of Nelson'. Although 'an old actor', this was almost his début as a vocalist.

Alfred Wigan's deteriorating health determined him to retire from management at the end of the season. His Farewell and Benefit on Friday, 24 July, was sponsored by an impressive Committee of Nobility and Gentry, which included Tennyson, Dickens, Richard Doyle, Planché, J. Palgrave Simpson and Tom Taylor.

Robson opened the evening with Miss Swanborough in *A Conjugal Lesson*; then came Tom Taylor's eighteenth-century costume piece ('from the French'), *A Sheep in Wolf's Clothing*.

At this point Wigan delivered his farewell speech, his right arm in a sling, 'with genuine and unaffected eloquence'. He paid a tribute to everyone in the theatre for their zealous and loyal co-operation, 'down to the humblest artisan'; he thanked his wife for having 'got up' ten pieces during his indisposition; he thanked the press for good and fair criticism. He was proud to think that the course he had adopted during his management had raised the Olympic to a high position in public favour 'as a place of rational, harmless entertainment'. Moreover, the Olympic also boasted a healthy balance sheet.

Mr. and Mrs. Wigan retired 'amid deafening cheers', and *Masaniello* concluded the evening. The last five nights of their lesseeship were devoted to *Daddy Hardacre* and *Masaniello*. What of the future? W. S. Emden, Acting Manager since the Wigans took over and previously at the Princess's, and Frederick Robson became joint lessees.

They took over the Olympic at a good moment in its fortunes. It had a much better reputation than at the beginning of the Wigan régime. The Wigans had succeeded where Farren had failed. John Coleman admitted that 'the sordid neighbourhood, the ancient and fishlike smell which permeated every corner of the building' remained, but the energy, elegance and good taste of the Wigan management had brought all London to Wych Street. 'Society pieces, such as *Plot and Passion*, *Still Waters* and *Retribution* had never been better acted.' The Wigans had assembled a talented company, and had trained them well.[56]

Above all, there was Robson. 'From the public point of view, Robson was the Olympic, and the Olympic was Robson'.[57] 'We go to see Robson', as Sala said, and the editor of *The Times* recommended him to visitors as one of the notable sights of London.[58]

In the summer of 1857 — the *Daddy Hardacre* summer — Robson appealed to a wide audience, including such literary gentlemen as Henry James, and 'watching Robson' at the Olympic was one of the chief recreations of William Morris, Dante Gabriel Rossetti and Burne-Jones when they were living within walking distance in Red Lion Square.[59]

At this time *The Illustrated London News* (16 August 1857) described Robson as a little dapper gentleman, very much under the middle height with a wide-awake, happy-looking face, a brilliant eye and a brisk lively manner. He is well-bred and intelligent, but his conversation presents nothing remarkable . . . one of the most unassuming men in his vanity-ridden profession . . .

The author of one of Robson's successes could hardly believe Robson was as pleased with the part written for him as he appeared to be. But Wigan said:

If you never saw the phenomenon before, you now behold in that little man a specimen of a perfectly unaffected actor; he almost puzzled me by his openness and candour, but I soon found them to be genuine . . . if there exists a man perfectly incapable of affectation it is Mr. Robson.

This tribute from Wigan, apparently dating from the last days of their collaboration, shows no trace of jealousy or misunderstanding, but the admission that he had been 'almost puzzled' by Robson's openness and candour shows perhaps the difference between the two men.

It shows Robson at a happy moment in his career, before the shadows closed-in. As for his modesty, G. A. Sala recalls that whenever he met him in the street he 'used to blush crimson' and retreat round the nearest corner as soon as possible, because Sala had written an eulogistic account of one of his performances. Sala 'brought him to bay' at last, and came to know him well. He considered that the nervousness and false shame which made him shy and retiring in private stood him in good stead upon the stage.

NOTES TO PART II

Farren

[1] Clement Scott: *The Drama Yesterday and To-day*, London 1889.
[2] *The Builder*, London, 22 December 1849; Raymond Mander and Joseph Mitchenson: *The Lost Theatres of London*, London 1968.
[3] For an account of this gentleman's career, see Malcolm Morley: *The Marylebone Theatre*, London 1960.
[4] G. A. Sala: *Robson*, London 1864.
[5] See David L. Rinear: 'From the Artificial towards the Real: The Acting of William Farren', *Theatre Notebook*, Vol. XXXI, Number 1, for an analysis of Farren's acting style.
[6] Sir Francis Burnand: 'A Genius Nearly Forgotten', *Britannia* Articles, September 1907.
[7] See Frederick Robson Junior's Declaration in Appendix.
[8] See (6) above.
[9] Alan Mackinnon: *The Oxford Amateurs*, London 1910.

[10] H. Crabb Robinson: *The London Theatre*, edited by Eiluned Brown, London, The Society for Theatre Research, 1966.

[11] Comparing the text of the so-called Fourth Edition, brought out for the Olympic in 1853, we find no difference in dialogue, lyrics, or tunes, but important differences in the title page and list of characters. The Olympic version is no longer called a 'Travestie', but 'Macbeth somewhat removed from the text of Shakespeare'. In the Strand edition the characters are listed without comment; the Olympic edition has a humorous description of each. In the Strand edition, costumes are described as 'OPTIONAL: consult the works of Simmons, Nathan, Canter'. *Macbeth Travestie* still stands at the top of each page of text; clearly the edition printed for the Strand was re-bound for the Olympic, with the extra pages needed for the amplified list of characters, Farren's notes on the costumes, and a new title page.

[12] Henry Morley: *Journal of a London Playgoer*, London 1891.

[13] Dutton Cook: 'Frederick Robson', *The Gentleman's Magazine*, June 1882.

[14] See (6) above.

[15] See (13) above.

[16] George Henry Lewes: *Dramatic Essays* (with John Forster), London 1896.

[17] See (12) above.

The Wigans

[18] *Saturday Review*, 23 February 1861.

[19] John Coleman: *Plays and Playwrights*, London 1888.

[20] *Ibid.*

[21] C. E. Pascoe, Ed.: *The Dramatic List*, 1880.

[22] Dutton Cook: 'Frederick Robson', *The Gentleman's Magazine*, June 1882.

[23] Henry Morley: *Journal of a London Playgoer*, Vol. 1, London 1891.

[24] See (22) above.

[25] *Letters of Charles Dickens*, edited by his sister-in-law, London 1893.

[26] George Henry Lewes (with John Forster): *Dramatic Essays*, London 1896.

[27] See (23) above.

[28] E. L. Blanchard: *Life and Reminiscences*, ed. Clement Scott, London 1912. See Appendix 3.

[29] H. Crabb Robinson: *The London Theatre*, edited by Eiluned Brown, London STR, 1966.

[30] Queen Victoria's theatrical tastes in general, and her liking for Frederick Robson in particular, can be read about in George Rowell's very entertaining: *Queen Victoria goes to the Theatre*, London 1978.

[31] Clement Scott: *The Drama Yesterday and To-day*, London 1899.

[32] *Dictionary of National Biography*.

[33] Enthoven Collection in the British Theatre Museum, quoted by permission.

[34] See (28) above.

[35] Letter in the Folger Shakespeare Library, Washington DC, quoted by permission.

[36] Introduction to *The Yellow Dwarf* in J. R. Planché: *Extravaganzas*, London 1879.

[37] G. A. Sala: Article in *The Train*, London 1857.

[38] Westland Marston: *Our Recent Actors*, London 1888.

[39] W. M. Rossetti: *Pre-Raphaelite Diaries and Letters*, London 1900.

[40] See (37) above.

[41] Henry James: *A Small Boy and others*, London 1911.

[42] See (28) above.

[43] Dr. Jane S. Stedman: 'From Dame to Woman: W. S. Gilbert and Theatrical Transvestism', *Victorian Studies*, September 1970.

[44] *Reminiscences of Macready*, ed. Sir Frederick Pollock, London 1875. (Letter of Mrs. Pollock of June 1856).

[45] See (25) above.

[46] Dr. G. L. M. Strauss: *Reminiscences of an Old Bohemian*, London 1880.

[47] Sir Francis Burnand: 'A Genius nearly Forgotten', August instalment of *Britannia*, London 1907.

[48] See (28) above.

[49] The story of the Windsor Theatricals Row is given in full by the present writer in *Theatre Notebook*, Vol. XXV, Autumn 1971. The correspondence is reproduced by permission of the Enthoven Collection, British Theatre Museum, and the Kean Collection, Folger Shakespeare Library, Washington DC. See also: Charles H. Shattuck: 'A Victorian Stage Manager', *Theatre Notebook*, Vol. XXII, Spring 1968.

[50] See (41) above.

[51] See (31) above.

[52] Austin Brereton: *The Life of Henry Irving*, London 1908.

[53] Seymour Hicks: *Twenty four years of an actor's life*, London 1910.

[54] See (29) above.

[55] H. Barton Baker: *History of the London Stage*, London 1909.

[56] John Coleman: *Fifty Years of an Actor's Life*, London 1904.

[57] See (22) above.

[58] See (37) above.

[59] J. W. Mackail: *Life of William Morris*, London 1922.

Part III

Robson and Emden:
1857-1864

1. *The New Management, and the Fool's Revenge; The Doge of Duralto and a Royal Wedding*

It was understood that, although Robson and Emden were Joint Lessees and Managers, W. S. Emden alone should deal with the business side, for which he had been largely responsible during the Wigan régime. There was also a 'sleeping partner', G. C. Bentinck, a lawyer and M.P., who negotiated a seven-year lease in the autumn of 1857. According to Emden's statement of 1864, the three of them paid nearly £4,000 for good-will, scenery, etc. (see Appendix 4).

There was no break between the old and the new régimes. The house was crowded on Monday, 10 August 1857. The private boxes presented an array of fashion hardly to be expected in August, and 'in one quiet corner were congregated Dickens, Mark Lemon, Thackeray and Wilkie Collins' to see the first professional performance of Wilkie Collins' *The Lighthouse,* first given at Dickens' house earlier in the year.

The curtain raiser was *TheSubterfuge,* played by Mrs. Stirling, George Vining and G. Murray to some applause. But the evening did not really get under way until Robson came before the curtain to speak an address written for him by Robert Brough. What he owed to the Olympic was aptly expressed:

. . . on this very stage
My home from infancy — not as to age —
I could walk when I came here — that's all one —
But here I felt my feet and learnt to run.

Alone in the familiar theatre he finds it has grown alarmingly large, just as a child left at home 'to mind the house' might feel the rooms vast and the responsibility great:

Ladies and gentlemen, that boy am I
They who as parents kind in art have stood for me
(Who never gave me aught but what was good for me)
Have left the house for many a day . . .
Well, I've been educated with propriety
I've passed four years in very good society.

He made graceful allusions to Mr. and Mrs. Wigan, and to Emden:

My anxious father and consid'rate mother
Have left *me* in the charge of my big brother
A steady youth with brain quite free from dizziness,
Who has for years attended to the business.

Laughter and enthusiastic applause followed, and then came *The Lighthouse,* the piece for which the 'literary gentlemen' had been waiting.

In a preliminary puff on 8 August, *The Illustrated London News* said that the part of Aaron Gourock (originally played by Dickens) was one 'entirely apart from any which Mr. Robson had played in Wych Street' and would enable the great star to do himself justice in a line which had not hitherto been open to him. But the critics were not unanimous as to his success in the part. *The Illustrated London News* could only say that his performance was 'marked by much refinement of detail on which Mr. Robson bestowed laudable elaboration'. Another critic thought that, although there were many marked and telling touches of nature, there were 'points' to which exception might be taken. Yet another described it as *Daddy Hardacre* at sea. The professional production was admired, and there was praise for the scenery of Messrs. Gray and Craven. Miss Swanborough was commended, and Miss Wyndham was considered to have advanced in her profession. The evening ended with *Masaniello.*

The Lighthouse, The Subterfuge, and *Masaniello* ran until 17 October, except for Wednesday, 7 October, when all theatres were closed by order of the Lord Chamberlain to mark a day of Prayer and Humiliation when 'the whole country' met 'to deplore in the presence of God the national visitation involved in the Indian Mutiny'. On 8 October *The Times* published the sermons preached in the principal London Churches to large congregations.

Robson was out of the bill for three weeks from 26 October with what was described on his return as 'hoarseness'. Absences due to indisposition were on the increase. His stage fright was to reach such a pitch that he would gnaw his arm until it bled, and cry piteously 'I dare not go on, I dare not go on!' until the prompter pushed him on to the stage. He ate as well as drank too much, according to Harwood Cooper.

In retrospect, we can see the change in management as marking a downward turn in his career, although he seemed at the height of his powers and had some of his greatest parts before him. Irksome though it might have been, Wigan's discipline was doubtless salutary. Now there was no one to direct or control him.

The curious episode which came to be known as 'The Waterloo Bridge Mystery and *The Fool's Revenge*' probably played a part in increasing his nervous tension, but would have had little effect had he not been already morbidly sensitive.

Between 1856 and 1859 Robson asked Tom Taylor to transform *Rigoletto* for him from an opera into a play, as he thought he 'saw himself' as the jester. He had probably seen Ronconi as Rigoletto at Covent Garden in May 1853. Rigoletto-without-music would not have seemed absurd in the mid-nineteenth century. When Verdi's opera was first performed, critics condemned the music and praised the drama, particularly the acting of Ronconi. Robson's ambition to play the part is understandable. Although not himself deformed, his big head and small body destined him to make people laugh for most of his career, 'esser buffone' like Rigoletto. Here was a tragic part in which his physique would be no drawback.[1] [2]

Tom Taylor found that Robson had never heard of Victor Hugo's *Le Roi s'amuse,* which Francesco Maria Piave had adapted for Verdi, turning Triboulet into Rigoletto. Tom Taylor was discouraging, saying that horrors tolerable in a musical dress would be 'intolerable' in a more naked stage form, and that even Victor Hugo's drama contained much that would not be acceptable to an English public. These 'horrors' were probably to be found in the climax of play and opera in which Triboulet-Rigoletto gloats over a sack in which he believes he will find the corpse of his daughter's seducer. He hears (off) the voice of the seducer singing

Souvent femme varie
Bien fol qui s'y fie

(in *Le Roi s'amuse)*
or

La donna è mobile

(in *Rigoletto)*
He pulls open the sack, and finds therein his daughter's almost lifeless body. Victor Hugo gives father and daughter a painful final scene, Verdi a beautiful duet.

Robson is unlikely to have shrunk from such 'horrors', and Daddy Hardacre with Gam-Bogie would have made this Rigoletto-without-music memorable, even though the audience would have missed the customary happy ending and moral tag.

But the squeamish Tom Taylor turned this last scene into something neither Victor Hugo nor Verdi's librettist would have recognised. Galeotto (Victor Hugo's King and Verdi's Duke) abducts the jester's daughter, with the jester's unsuspecting connivance, but is then poisoned by his wife. She means to kill the girl also, but gives her a less than fatal dose and she recovers. The girl assures her father that she has not suffered 'wrong worse than death' (Tom Taylor's words), but is as pure as when she last kissed his lips. She is neither seduced nor murdered, and the curtain falls on a tableau of repentance. This is a pleasanter ending than *Le Roi s'amuse* or *Rigoletto,* but dramatically less effective. Phelps, however, made a success of it, and it was later one of Edwin Booth's great parts. But it was not the part in which Robson had 'seen himself'.[3]

Besides altering the ending Tom Taylor was inspired to write the English version in blank verse, which he gives as an additional reason for Robson's refusal, since the Olympic was not associated with verse drama.

Hollingshead also tells us that Tom Taylor prepared Triboulet for Robson, who was already haunted by a fear of failure, crying constantly 'Can I keep it up? Can I keep it up?', and who was shocked by the Waterloo Bridge mystery into refusing the part, A 'Greenacre Bag' * on the stage of the Olympic would 'Never do', and so the part went to Phelps at Sadlers Wells, not so near to the Waterloo Bridge.[4]

What was the mystery? The press for mid-October 1857, supplemented by Elliott O'Donnell's researches, tells the story.[5] On Friday, 9 October 1857, two boys who were rowing up the Thames found a locked carpet bag lying on its side on the third abutment of Waterloo Bridge. It was found to contain human remains and blood-stained clothing. The Police took the bag to Bow Street, and an inquest was held in the Board Room of the Strand Union on Monday, 12 October. The room was crowded and many people from the neighbourhood assembled outside. Among them must have been regular patrons of the Olympic, and probably some of the actors. Those who lived south of the river and had to cross the Bridge on their way to and from the

---

*In 1827 a murderer called Greenacre chopped up his victim's remains and put them in a bag, and similar crimes were thereafter known as Greenacre Bag murders. The sack in the last act of *Rigoletto* was therefore a kind of 'Greenacre Bag'.

theatre, either on foot (paying the halfpenny toll) or in an omnibus, must have felt a *frisson* at the evidence of the toll-keeper:

> I was on duty last Thursday night at half-past eleven. I remember seeing a woman come up from the Strand side . . . She had a carpet bag . . . Her hair looked as if it had been powdered or plastered on her forehead . . . She spoke rather gruffly; it was certainly in a masculine tone of voice. Her height might have been about five feet three inches.

A second witness, approaching from the north side, had followed the woman and commented that her hair did not look natural. Here, on the Bridge which Frederick Robson traversed daily, was a short man dressed as a woman with hair plastered on the forehead in a theatrical manner.

We are not suggesting that anyone seriously connected Robson with the Waterloo Bridge mystery. But to him, already doubting his capacity to sustain the part of the jester and perhaps already giving thought to the last scene in which he has to open and gloat over a bag of human remains, the coincidence must have been disturbing. To play such a scene at the Olympic, so close to the Waterloo Bridge, while the events were fresh in people's minds, would have been distressing and embarrassing at least.

As Hollingshead put it, the Waterloo Bridge mystery had 'frightened him', and he refused the part. It seems probable that Tom Taylor's alteration of the last act also was influenced by the Waterloo Bridge mystery, and that he too decided that the 'Greenacre Bag' was not suitable to the stage.

Regret that Robson never played the jester is tempered by the knowledge that Tom Taylor's emasculated version would not have given him the part he wanted.

The Mystery was never solved.

After his return on 10 November with his 'late hoarseness partially cured' Robson's first new part was Mr. Samuel Todd/Signor Toddini in Stirling Coyne's *What will they say at Brompton?* — a farce considerably less silly than most. Mr. Todd and his wife, who live at Cosey Cottage, Brompton, decide to go to Italy for their holiday, instead of the usual Gravesend or Margate. The night before their departure, Mr. Todd soothes his travel nerves with an opium cigar; this produces fantastic dreams, in which he becomes Signor Toddini, in love with a brigand's sister, living in a ruined castle in the Alps. Various inconsequent episodes occur, culminating in an attack upon the castle and a fire . . . after which Mr. Toddini/Todd wakes up in Cosey Cottage:

Mr. Robson's impersonation of the affrighted cockney in the robbers' retreat was perfect in its way; and nothing could be finer than the transition from the troubadour lover, all gaiety and fun, to the miserable conscience-stricken husband. (*Observer*).

The Times praised not only Robson, but also Mr. Addison as a bluff brigand chief and Mr. G. Cooke cleverly made-up as the croaking old uncle. It was not often that these hard-working actors were individually mentioned, and is evidence of the good ensemble which had been built-up around the star.

R. B. Brough's *Doge of Duralto* amused the Christmas audiences, but did little to enhance the reputation of Robson or the Olympic. The confused story had some originality: Impecunioso XXI (Robson) has a step-daughter whose every tear is a pearl, so he shuts her up and ill-treats her in order that he may garner the fruits of her misery. John Oxenford thought the character was merely 'Daddy Hardacre slightly burlesqued', and lamented that 'the most successful actor of the day' should display his peculiar powers in something so 'uncommonly flat'. Robson parodied *King Lear, A New Way to Pay Old Debts,* and *Macbeth,* and sang burlesque versions of 'Hoop de denda doo' and 'The Lost Child'. The weight of the piece was on his shoulders, although Miss Wyndham as the Princess and Miss Hughes as Ulfo were praised. The piece was 'very well-mounted', with scenery by J. Gray and H. Craven, and the 'attention to minor accessories' showed the hand of a careful stage-manager, W. S. Emden; *The Times* praised the music, including the 'Laughing Song' from *The Rose of Castile,* the inevitable 'Parigi o Cara', etc., but the *Illustrated London News* thought the selection poor.

It was received with applause, but also some expressions of disapproval, warning Robson that 'his patrons would not be content with a continual round of food for children'. In *Crinoline,* which followed, Robson did not appear, and Horace Wigan played Nancy Bitters, the part in which James Rogers had made his unfortunate gag.

The marriage of 'England's Eldest Daughter', Victoria, to Crown Prince Frederick William of Prussia was celebrated by lavish fetes, balls and banquets in the winter of 1857-1858. There was some murmuring among the poor and those who ministered to them. 'An East End Incumbent' reminded the supposedly wealthy readers of *The Times* of the poor, destitute and starving in the metropolis whose outdoor relief was a shilling a week and a loaf, and of the 100,000 in the workhouses on the wedding day. Could not the workhouse dinners be at least improved, and some contribution in money given to the outdoor poor?

In the London theatres there were four festival performances, in the second of which Robson and his colleagues took part. On Thursday, 1 January, the programme at Her Majesty's Theatre consisted of Balfe's opera *The Rose of Castile,* performed by the Lyceum Company, and *Boots at the Swan* by the Olympic: Robson was supported by Mesdames Cotterell, Castleton, Emden and Evans, and Messrs. George Murray, George Vining and Horace Wigan. The opera began at half-past seven, and was followed by a long interval, and then the singing of the National Anthem. It must have been late when the curtain rose upon the farce; this had allowed the Olympic Company to play a 'Juvenile Night' in their own theatre, timed to end at 10.30.

When *Boots at the Swan* finally appeared, 'Mr. Robson was as usual irresistibly funny, and kept the audience, Royal visitors and all, in fits of laughter'. *The Times* wrote:

> The impression produced upon the occupants of the Queen's Box, including Her Majesty herself, by the inimitable drollery of Mr. Robson as the deaf Boots, baffles description. The roars of laughter which proceeded from the house, at each diverting stroke of humour, could hardly have been more cheering to the actor than the less vehemently expressed, but not a bit less genial and unconstrained hilarity of Her Majesty and her distinguished circle of relatives and friends.

The 'distinguished circle' had occupied 17 state carriages, escorted by a detachment of Life Guards, and included the bride, her parents, an impressive contingent of Hohenzollerns, and 'Uncle Leopold', King of the Belgians.

The wedding over and the Princess now established in her adopted country, the Queen wrote to her about a visit on 6 February to the Olympic to see Robson in *The Doge of Duralto;* he was 'very good', and Miss Wyndham as 'the Princess who cries pearls was very amusing'.[6] [7]

On 15 February the Royal Box was occupied by the Duchess of Cambridge to see *The Doge.* These Royal visits were announced on forms printed in copperplate delivered to the Manager of the theatre to be honoured:

> Sir Charles Phipps presents his compliments to . . . and begs to inform him that the Queen's Box at the . . . will be occupied by . . . this evening.

Boots and *The Doge* ran together, but on 8 March Robson had a new part in a costume farce by J. M. Morton, *Ticklish Times,* set in

Weymouth in 1750. Sir William Ramsay, a Jacobite leader (Walter Gordon), seeking to escape to the continent with his wife, passes himself off as 'Lancelot Griggs'. The real Griggs (Robson) appears, but Sir William continues to bluff it out: 'Griggs I am, and Griggs I must remain until I have provided for my safety'. The real Griggs' bewilderment at this usurpation of his name and identity was the kind of thing Robson did so well; with gesture, vocal inflection and facial expression he appealed to the sympathy of the audience. Further misunderstandings occur before Ramsay escapes, and Griggs is restored to his rightful personality. Played with pace and good timing, with Robson at his most whimsical and the beautiful Louisa Herbert as Lady Ramsay, this farce ran for 71 performances. It was subsequently revived from time to time, and was the last play in which Robson appeared at the Olympic. Queen Victoria saw it on 4 April.

On 5 June Robson took his Benefit, the main piece being Tom Taylor's *Going to the Bad*, 'a new and original comedy in two acts'. Peter Potts (Robson) flirts with Miss Dashwood (Miss Herbert), who rebuffs him; he gets drunk and belligerent; he goes to a fancy ball as Mephistopheles; he plans to fight a duel . . . But a series of improbable explanations brings everything to a satisfactory close. Almost the whole of the company was engaged in this romp, which ran for a month.

2. *The Red Vial; The Porter's Knot; Payable on Demand; and others*

The season which opened on 18 September had nothing new for Robson until the unfortunate *Red Vial* by Wilkie Collins on 11 October.

After its first performance by the Tavistock House amateurs on 16 June 1855, Wilkie Collins set about negotiating a professional production. Webster of the Haymarket 'nibbled', but withdrew. Alfred Wigan was approached, but he felt unable to cast the principal part, which really required 'a first-rate serious actor'.[8] Unwisely, Robson and Emden decided to undertake it, with Robson in the 'difficult' part of Hans Grimm, the half-witted dwarf.

It was indeed a heavy-handed melodrama. Madame Bergmann (Mrs. Stirling) has stolen money from her employer, Isaac Rodenberg (Mr. Addison), and wants to marry her daughter to Rodenberg's partner, Karl. She fears her theft will be discovered and the marriage prevented, so she pours deadly poison from a red vial into Rodenberg's lemonade. Hans Grimm, the half-wit (Robson), observes her, and while she is not looking pours an antidote into the lemonade. She believes Rodenberg to be already dead, but he enters (clad in a black pall) and forces her to drink a few fatal drops from her own red vial.

Blanchard describes the drama as 'extraordinary', to which Clement Scott adds a footnote saying that Robson was 'great', though some blamed Robson for the failure. Hollingshead and Sergeant Ballantyne blamed nothing but the piece, even though Robson was 'not quite what he was'.

'On the first night it was damned', said the author, 'Mrs. Stirling and Addison admirable. Poor little Robson did his best. The rest is silence'.[9] Damned or not, *The Red Vial*, ran for four weeks bolstered by *To Oblige Benson* and *Ladies Beware*.

On 15 November there was a revival of Morton's early farce *A Thumping Legacy*, in which Robson had made his first appearance in Dublin in 1850. A cockney druggist, known as Jerry Ominous, descended from the ancient Corsican family of Geronimo, goes to Corsica to claim 'a thumping legacy', said to have been left by an uncle. The uncle is still alive, and has lured Jerry to Corsica to make him kill a member of a rival family, to revenge an hereditary wrong. J. L. Toole compares Robson's and Keeley's readings of the phrase 'Don't you think we had better take a chair?'. Keeley was quiet, whereas Robson was all excitement, and spoke the lines in a tragic tone.[10] Jerry was

. . . one of those personations of cockney shrewdness and cockney pusillanimity that are likewise adapted to Mr. Robson. He is perpetually in a state of terror, but is never frightened out of his wits . . . Perfectly in his element, and embellishing the dialogue with all sorts of chimerical conceits, Mr. Robson kept the house in a roar . . .

Miss Herbert, Mr. Gordon and Mr. Horace Wigan were 'perfect representatives of a picturesque ferocity', and Mr. G. Cooke played the uncle with much power. Scenery and costumes were also praised.

John Oxenford's adaptation of a French original, *Les Crochets du Père Martin*, under the name of *The Porter's Knot*, was produced on 2 December. This gave Robson one of his most famous parts. The play is set in a seaside town resembling Whitstable. Samson Burr, the old porter, has retired after years of honest toil, the proceeds of which have enabled his son to train as a doctor. But the son has involved himself in debts of £2,000. The old porter pretends that he himself has lost this sum, hoping to shield the boy and protect the old mother from suffering. He returns to his job as porter.

E. L. Blanchard thought *The Porter's Knot* exquisitely acted by Robson and the rest, and H. Crabb Robinson considered the exhibition of 'passion in his paternal affliction unique'.[11] [12] It was considered very touching and sweet by Marston, and H. Barton Baker only qualified his praise by saying that it was 'somewhat strained and maw-kish'.[13] [14] Clement Scott said:

> I see now through the mist of years Robson sitting on his truck with Mrs. Leigh Murray by his side, eating the dinner the good wife had brought down to the pier for her proud old husband, lamenting over their poor lost boy. But the prodigal returns, well and prosperous, able to pay back his 'dear Daddy' the money that has been wasted on his folly. The reconciliation between father and son as played by Robson was one of the most affecting things I ever saw on the stage. The audience did not cry; it alternately sobbed and howled.[15]

Yet deeply as Robson undoubtedly felt 'the passions of the men he was impersonating', when he and his prodigal son met in their heart-rending embrace, and the whole house was 'snivelling, weeping and coughing', Robson would say to Walter Gordon: 'Walter, my boy, I wonder what's for supper to-night? I wonder if it's tripe?'.[16] Clement Scott compares this with Ellen Terry's occasional practical jokes at moments of high dramatic tension.

Samson Burr seems a dramatic world away from the absurd Signor Toddini or Jerry Ominous, and from the sinister Yellow Dwarf or Prince Richcraft. Samson Burr was all simple goodness and whimsical humour, like Dickens at his cosiest. There were indeed contradictions in Robson the actor similar to those in Dickens the writer. In humour, pathos and horror alike he could be called a Dickensian actor. He had played Sarah Gamp and Young Bailey at the Grecian, but what a Quilp he would have made, what a Uriah Heep, but also what a Sam Weller, or even Pickwick, with some padding. Dickens and Robson appealed to the same public.

The Porter's Knot ran until Christmas, with *A Thumping Legacy* to provide laughter after the tears.

On Boxing Day Robson was back to absurdity in *Mazeppa*, J. J. Byron's burlesque of the Astley equestrian drama. The tune of 'Barbara Allen' was used for the first and last numbers; in between the arrangers drew upon opera *(The Bronze Horse, Ernani, La Sonnambula)* and minstrel ditties. A writer in the *Referee* of 10 August 1903 said he had remembered from childhood Robson's singing of

> Had it not been for Olinska
>   That very lovely gal
> Her father would have sent me
>   To the Foundling Hospital.

(Tune: 'The Nigger's History')

102

His 'bareback riding' on a Lowther Arcade rocking-horse was one of the great effects of the evening. The little malacca cane he used is still preserved by his descendants. But the exertion of the ride proved too much for him when he was playing *The Porter's Knot* the same evening. On 5 January *The Doge* was substituted for *Mazeppa*.

The Porter's Knot with other supporting pieces ran until the end of the season, with only two breaks, one in Holy Week and the other in mid-January, explained by the strain of this ride in *Mazeppa* in the following terms:

The Porter's Knot will shortly be repeated, the physical exertion required for the extravaganza not permitting Mr. Robson to appear in the two pieces in the same evening.

But familiarity with Mazeppa soon allowed of his playing both roles in one programme, which he did for five weeks, after which *Mazeppa* was dropped. Mazeppa had been an exacting part:

Mazeppa, while on the back of his steed, describes in a series of puns his sufferings, but when off, becomes a maniac, fancying himself to be a rider at Astley's, and this affords Robson the opportunity of a great triumph.

During Holy Week the theatre was occupied by the German Reeds, with their *Popular Illustrations from Real Life*.

On 17 May, the 108th night of *The Porter's Knot,* a new farce by John Oxenford was brought out — *Retained for the Defence*. Pawkins, a cockney barber, accused of stealing a watch, was a part tailored to Robson's comic talents, and he modelled him on one Cubitt, a barber of Oakley Street (now Baylis Street) known to himself and Harwood Cooper. Acquitted after a brilliant defence by his Counsel, Mr. Whitewash (George Vining), he is invited to a party to celebrate the outcome. The little man is bewildered 'between the ices and the ladies'; eating ices was a new and not very pleasurable experience, and 'you could positively feel the pain that Pawkins was supposed to be feeling as, with a semi-tragical, semi-comical countenance, he said: 'Right in the holler!'.[17] Crabb Robinson said that nothing Liston performed was so farcical as Robson's Pawkins:

. . . His grimaces at seeing *hice* at a *swarry,* and the way in which he 'olds his *umbrelli* and *vipes* his nose defy all criticism.

At the last rehearsal Oxenford was despondent and feared a failure: 'However, boys, do your best for me!' was his final exhortation according to Harwood Cooper, and they certainly did.

These two contrasting characters of Oxenford's — the honest old

Kentish porter and the ludicrous cockney barber — were played together until the end of the first week of July. It was in that week that Crabb Robinson walked to the theatre and saw both.

On 11 July Robson played a part utterly different from either — Reuben Goldsched in Tom Taylor's *Payable on Demand.*

The play, suggested by the real life story of the Rothschilds, opens in the Goldsched home in the Frankfurt ghetto in 1792. The Marquis de St. Cast, a royalist escaping from the revolutionary armies, entrusts a large sum of money to Reuben, which the Jew hides in the cradle of his sleeping babe. The soldiers search the house, but respect the babe's slumbers. The Marquis has written in invisible ink a receipt for the money and places it in the secret drawer of a Buhl writing-desk he happens to be carrying beneath his cloak. He is killed (off), and Reuben is tempted to forget about the receipt, but his wife makes him swear to keep the money in trust for the rightful heir. He swears on his father's Old Testament, propped at the head of the cradle; his wife clasps her hands in thanksgiving and the curtain falls.

Act II shows Reuben, now a widower, living prosperously at Clapham, having made a fortune by clever speculation. The markets go up and down with the fortunes of war. The innocent babe is now a fair young maiden (played by Miss Wyndham, the mother in Act I). She has fallen in love with a poor young music-master, really the son of the late Marquis de St. Cast (Walter Gordon, who was the father in Act I). The Buhl desk turns up, and in the secret drawer they find the paper which, when held to the light, proves to be the receipt 'Payable on Demand'. The war news is critical. If Reuben gives the Marquis's son his rightful due he may be ruined. But he conquers the temptation to keep the money. Virtue is rewarded. A carrier pigeon brings the intelligence of Napoleon's defeat. The stocks rise, and the young people are united.

Robson gave the audience their money's worth of sudden transitions, hysterical outbursts and paternal affection. Squire Bancroft wrote:

> When the news of the battle of Waterloo was brought to him by carrier pigeon, he ran round the room embracing it, and covering it with kisses in a way which provoked no smile, only applause.[18]

The situations were described as 'picturesque' by the *Illustrated London News;* 'an oriental colouring was thrown over the action, and the character of the Jew brought into relief by costume and accessories'. The dresses (carefully in period) were by S. May, and the scenery by W. Telbin.

This serio-comic drama, as the author called it, ran until the end of the season, and was included in an Extra Night for the Benefit of Conway, the prompter — a gentleman very necessary to Robson as his memory deteriorated.

As reported in the *Morning Chronicle* of 22 August, Mr. Robson addressed the audience on the last night, 'humorously reviewing the principal events of the management during the year':

> You apparently have been very pleased with us; at any rate you have given us very substantial reasons for believing so, and we, as a matter of course, are extremely grateful to you. Shall I tell you the truth, without reservation or disguise? I know that I am among friends, who will not abuse my confidence. Well, then, we have had a very excellent season, and we are in such high spirits on account of the past, that we are not a little sanguine with respect to the future.

3. *Alfred the Great; and a Personal Interlude*

At the end of August 1859 Robson was back in Dublin, at the Queen's, for the first time for three years, 'supported' by Olympic colleagues: Miss Hughes, Messrs. Gordon, Murray, Cooke and Conway. They played *The Porter's Knot, Boots, Pawkins the Persecuted (Retained for the Defence), Medea, Daddy Hardacre* and some other pieces in which Robson did not appear. The last night in Dublin was Saturday, 9 September.

The Olympic was re-opened on Saturday, 24 September. Emden and Robson remained joint lessees and managers; Horace Wigan, Assistant Stage Manager, later 'Stage Director'; scenery supervised by Mr. Telbin; music, Mr. Barnard; dances, Mr. Milano; machinery, Mr. Sutherland; properties and decorations, Mr. Lightfoot; dresses, Mr. S. May and Mrs. Curl; wigs, Mr. Clarkson. There was a large audience for *Morning Call* (Mrs. Stirling and George Vining), followed by the 36th performance of *Payable on Demand* and the 56th of *Retained for the Defence*.

On 17 October *Payable on Demand* was 'unavoidably' withdrawn with no explanation; *The Porter's Knot* was revived, and on 7 November Robson appeared as Medea for the first time for three years. Jason was played by Miss Wyndham until 19 November, when she was replaced at the last moment by Miss Eliza Nelson; Addison was Creon; Miss Hughes, Orpheus; the ever-useful Harwood Cooper 'a Corinthian', and Miss Cotterell, Creusa. The house was full.

Horace Wigan's new farce 'from the French', *The Head of the*

Family, and T. H. Bayly's *Tom Noddy's Secret* had no parts for Robson. Mesdames Cotterell, Hughes, Marston, Herbert and Emden (with occasionally Mrs. Stirling), and Messrs. G. Cooke, G. and F. Vining, Harwood Cooper and Horace Wigan were a good company, but the public expected to see Robson at least once every evening. They were kept going with *Medea* and *Retained for the Defence* until Boxing Day, when Robert Brough's new 'Historical Extravaganza' of *King Alfred the Great* was produced.

The general theme was burlesque patriotism. Puns abounded, and there were more topical allusions than usual in such pieces — among others to army reform, the Strike Fund, the laying of the Atlantic Cable, the poet Bunn, Sidney Carton, the auction of what remained of Vauxhall Gardens, and Professor Blondin's crossing of Niagara. Mr. Barnard 'arranged' a variety of popular airs, including some minstrel tunes such as 'I'm off to Charleston', operatic arias from *Dinorah, I Puritani* and *Fra Diavolo,* and patriotic songs such as 'The Death of Nelson' and 'Rule Britannia'. The singing strength of the Olympic was good, it seems, since the book of the play provides that the aria from *I Puritani* could be replaced by the 'familiar melody', 'Dusty Sot', by non-operatic companies.

The audience responded with delight to the idea of little Robson posing as a national hero. Somehow the Wizard Merlin and the witches' cauldron from *Macbeth* turned up in the Goatherd's cottage, and among the apparitions was 'a small government clerk with a huge piece of red tape in his hands', and a small sailor with a model of the new Victoria ship.

E. L. Blanchard found it 'went very slow; good lines, but construction queer'.[19] Queen Victoria thought Robson 'charming'. Her half-sister, Princess Feodora of Leiningen, occupied the Royal Box on 12 February, after visiting Westminster Abbey and 'the new Palace of Westminster' in the afternoon.

In November Queen Victoria had commanded *To Oblige Benson* at Windsor, with Robson of course.

In the late autumn of 1859 (according to the Declaration of Maria Bailey, the housemaid) Frederick Robson moved from Kennington Park to 19 Ampthill Square, Camden Town, where he was to live until his death in August 1864. He had paid the rates from September 1859, but his new address did not appear on the playbills until January 1860.

The Square — really a triangle — lay to the east of the Hampstead Road, and had been only recently developed from open fields. It is now replaced by a housing estate. The Hampstead Road, though in appearance much changed, still links Tottenham Court Road with

Camden Town High Street, and ultimately with Hampstead and High-gate. Many of the shopfronts in the High Street conceal houses which must have been there in Robson's time and earlier. The statue of Cobden was erected by subscription not long before his death. Nearby Oakley Square remains, where Dr. Andrews lived, Robson's doctor in his last illness and witness to his Will. But St. Matthew's Church — where Fanny Robson and Robert Charles Brookes were married in 1871, and E. M. Robson and Elizabeth Smith in 1874 — was demolished in 1976.

Why did he move from his almost native South London? Perhaps he wanted a better house for his children, with a good garden. J. L. Toole, who lived at one time in Hampstead and was a keen gardener, thought that the cure for Robson's nervousness and restlessness would have been 'a little gardening':

> He was fidgety and restless sometimes on the stage, but always off, and I noticed that after we had sat in the summer house for a time, with an occasional prowl on the grass, a sniff at a Gillyflower or a bit of London Pride, he would settle down like a man who is resting, grow quiet and reflective, and we would have a calm and enjoyable chat.[20]

There was a good garden at the back of the house, as well as a communal garden in the centre of the Square. J. L. Toole may well have been right, but by this time it was too late for Robson to change; his restlessness and self-distrust were pushing him to resort more and more to alcohol rather than gardening for relief.

The distance to the Olympic was slightly less than from Kennington, if he went by brougham — his own, according to Harwood Cooper, hired, according to Francis Burnand. W. S. Emden had moved from Tavistock Street to Upper Park Road, Hampstead, in 1860. This was about a mile north of Ampthill Square. Harwood Cooper remained south of the river, in Tenison Street, Lambeth.

Another South London friendship was with George Shipman; he followed Robson across the river and lived just round the corner from Ampthill Square in the Hampstead Road. Robson lent him money to start a cigar shop. In 1861 he was 'painter and glazier' but in 1862 he had become 'Tobacconist'. Shipman, it will be recalled, had been one of the Amateurs of the Bower, had promoted the little Eccentric Club in Hercules Buildings; and was a friend of Claudius May, Robson's brother-in-law. Robson's delight was to associate with Brookes at 'the Shop' (his surgery) and Shipman at the Cigar Shop on a Sunday evening. He did not like to be thought a 'Society Man'; he clearly enjoyed the company of those not in the acting profession, but started his brougham so that he could wave his hand at early acquaintances who wished to congratulate him on his success (and possibly cadge favours), instead of having to ask them to lunch. Yet he was faithful to old friends, professional or otherwise, and had no snobbery.

Of these friends the most notable were the Brookes, a family which had belonged to Lambeth for generations. Eighteenth-century Brookeses were buried in St. Mary's, where Robson was married and Harwood Cooper baptised. They were a family of doctors, and the friendship may have originated in a doctor-patient relationship. Charles Brookes had his 'shop' or surgery at 57 Mount Street, Lambeth. In 1853 he gave a copy of Shakespeare's plays to Robson; this was the year of the Olympic début. In December 1859 Robson wrote to 'C.B., Esq.' on Olympic notepaper asking if his 'young friend' Master Brookes would like a box for the last appearance of 'Mrs. Medea' on Friday, 23 December. A postscript says 'Oh, this Christmas work!', alluding to the preparations for *Alfred*. There were three 'Master Brookeses' — Walter, Frederick and Robert Charles, who married Fanny Robson in 1871 (see Appendix 1). All three became doctors.

The Brookes family remained in South London, but the friendship was not affected by Robson's move. In 1861 a Doulton wine jug was presented by 'C.B.' to his sincere friend F.R.'. The silver lid bears a figure of Bacchus straddling a barrel, and the hinge is surmounted by a nymph holding a bunch of grapes. That a doctor should give Robson further encouragement in the worship of Bacchus seems strange, but possibly Charles Brookes wished to encourage him to drink wine rather than spirits.[21]

Maria Bailey the housemaid (then Maria Tanner) says in her Declaration that she accompanied 'Mr. Robson and his family' in the move (see Appendix 2: The Paternity of E. M. Robson). Young Frederick says that he and his sister went to live with their father in the new home, whereas when he lived in Kennington they were sent to various boarding-schools. Fanny went to boarding-school in Edinburgh for a while, where she learnt genteel accomplishments, including riding and the serving of thin bread-and-butter on At Home Days.[22]

Neither Maria nor Frederick tells us of what 'Mr. Robson's family' then consisted. But the March 1861 Census Return shows a lady with the Christian names of 'Sarah E.' claiming to be the wife of the head of the household, with two sons, 'Henry A.' aged 17 and 'Frederick' aged 16, and two daughters, 'Fanny' aged 14 and 'Mary E.' aged 12.

'Henry A.' and 'Mary E.' must have been 'Sarah E.'s' own children. Young Frederick Robson was 17, not 16, at this time, the same age as her own son. A photograph about 1860 shows Robson seated, with a youth resembling later photographs of 'young Fred' standing behind his chair, and two little girls, about the same height and dressed alike in the style of Alice-in-Wonderland, in front of the actor; one is leaning against him, and the other seems to be pulling away, shyly or crossly. One is presumably Fanny Robson and the other 'Mary E'.

'Sarah E.', who claimed to be Mrs. Robson in 1861, and whose children were apparently being brought up with his, has been identified by Mr. F. Renad Cooper as Sarah Emma Humphrey, daughter of a coach wheelwright of William Street, St. Pancras, married to Charles Philip Manly of the same street on 11 May 1842.

When did she and Robson set up house together, and was she 'the old woman' who was in 'a towering passion' when the sheets were dyed yellow by the Yellow Dwarf make-up? We are unlikely ever to find the answer to these questions.

Wherever she came from and however long their association, she and her children disappeared from the Robson 'family' soon after the Census return. Young Fred tells us he endeavoured to bring about a reconciliation between his parents, and eventually succeeded. Maria Bailey tells us that between 1859 and the summer of 1861 she was asked to send a money order to a Mrs. Brownbill at Hackney, and on another occasion was sent to Hackney where she saw Mrs. Brownbill and a little boy with 'hair inclined to be carrotty', called Edwin May, about six or seven years old. He was said to be her nephew. Some time after this, Mr. Robson was ill, and Mrs. Brownbill came to Ampthill Square, and 'saw him in the drawing-roon'.[23] This must have been between 20 May and 10 June, when he was absent from the Olympic with 'a severe indisposition'.

'Some few months subsequently' Mrs. Brownbill came again, and remained, but she did not bring Edwin May with her. This reconciliation must have been in late summer or early autumn 1861. Maria herself was married from the house in January 1862, and went to live at Carshalton as Mrs. Bailey. Edwin May was sent to her several times 'for holidays', and Mr. Robson and his family also visited her several times. In his *Who's Who in the Theatre* entry E. M. Robson speaks of being 'educated' at Bexley Heath, presumably at boarding-school, and this was the period when he spent holidays with Mrs. Maria Bailey. Previous to that, he seems to have been boarded out, since young Frederick remembers being taken to see him by his mother, and giving him a present of money.

Rosetta Brownbill's version of these events in her Declaration is disingenuous. She says her husband 'returned' to her in the year 1861, and continued to live with her and her children until his death. But Ampthill Square was *his* home, and *she* joined *him*. For the first year, Edwin May was not part of the household. Not until young Fred was away from home, acting in the provinces, did she introduce Edwin May into the family. She maintains that Robson always recognised him as his son, and never denied that he was their lawful child. Robert Charles Brookes, on the other hand, a professional man of undoubted integrity, says that Edwin always called Robson 'Uncle' and Mrs. Robson 'Aunt', and that Robson never showed any affection towards the child in his presence. His Will spoke of two children only.[24]

The best we can say for Rosetta Brownbill, now known as Mrs. Robson, is that between the signing of the Will and his death Frederick Robson may have grown fond of the child, as he guided his first steps on the stage in *Medea* (see below). *The Era* of 21 August 1864 speaks of 'his nephew of whom he was very fond'. The question of his paternity is more fully discussed in Appendix 2.

The motive for Rosetta's reconciliation with her husband is hard to judge. There may have been a revival of affection for him, and for her two elder children; or she may have wanted security. He was quite a celebrity now, with a good house and two servants.

This then was Robson's home background for the last three years of his Olympic career: a comfortable home in a new suburb, shared first with Mrs. Manly and her two children, as well as his own; then with his formerly estranged wife and their two children, until young Fred went out into the world, when a so-called nephew was introduced. In 1863 they all four went on tour together, apparently on good terms.

Some time in 1862 Squire Bancroft, then acting in the Birmingham Company to which 'young Fred' was a recent recruit, went to London to see the Exhibition, and was presented to the 'great-little Robson'. Bancroft had been 'enthralled' by Robson in *The Porter's Knot, Plot and Passion, Payable on Demand,* and so on, and thought him the most remarkable actor of those times, perhaps of any time. 'No words of mine could do justice to my remembrance of this strange little genius', he said. On the occasion of this visit, Robson showed him some framed engravings of actors, and of one of them said: 'That was one of the cleverest and most natural comedians I ever saw'. This was Edward Pierce, Christy Minstrel, and first singer of 'Hoop de denda'.[25]

Among other theatre people who visited 19 Ampthill Square was Edward Fitzball, who wrote verses in Fanny Robson's Album to celebrate her sixteenth birthday, addressing her as 'Young lovely rose of Ampthill Square'.

4. *B.B. and its rehearsal*

There were still some good things to come. John Oxenford's 'new' *Uncle Zachary*, founded on *L'Oncle Baptiste*, was 'a rich treat for Robson's admirers'. Uncle Zachary and his wife Tabitha (Mrs. Leigh Murray) are honest folk who have come in to some money, and wish to share their luck with their relatives, particularly with a niece who is about to be married. Unfortunately, her betrothed has a very snobbish uncle, and their arrival at the wedding is a disaster, especially when Uncle Zachary gets very drunk. However, all ends well, when Uncle Zachary discovers the snobbish uncle is an old friend of humble origin. The *Morning Chronicle* said:

> One moment the most ludicrous presentation of the drunkard, and the next a most touching mixture of anger and sorrow . . . the whole character is one which, although it may have been equalled, has never been surpassed by Mr. Robson himself.

Uncle Zachary ran for 80 performances, well on into June. It was joined on 30 March by *B.B.*, a farce written jointly by Montagu Williams and Francis Burnand.

According to Harwood Cooper, the manuscript was first read by the managers rather hastily, and rejected. But the once famous Mrs. Keeley called upon Emden in his private room and begged him to re-read her son-in-law's play. She said:

> I have brought it with me. I was so pleased with it that I was the party that suggested sending it to you for Robson, who I can see in the character — take my advice, Emden, produce it, and you won't regret having done so.

The two Managers re-read it, Robson discovered the comicality of the character and it was produced.

The prize fight between Tom Sayers, the Englishman, and John C. Heenan, the American or 'Benicia Boy', produced a crop of farces about this time, of which *B.B.* was one. Mr. Benjamin Bobbin arrives at the Percy Arms and is mistaken for the Benicia Boy, who is to fight the British champion. At the heart of all the farcical misunderstandings was Robson as Benjamin Bobbin, supported by Horace Wigan as Bob Rattles, a retired prize fighter; George Cooke as Squire Greenfield; Harwood Cooper as Joe; Mrs. Stephens as the landlady; and Mrs. Emden as the housemaid. 'Supported' is the right word; in this play the others had to be subordinate, yet always ready to adapt themselves to Robson's changes of business.

Burnand's own account of the rehearsals gives us a unique picture of

Robson's method of working and of behind the scenes at the Olympic. Burnand already had some burlesques to his credit, but Montagu Williams, somewhat senior to him at Eton, was a novice as a playwright. Both were too bewildered to interfere in the almost chaotic proceedings. In later years, Burnand was to rehearse his own works very carefully and to be inventive in stage business. Dr. Jane Stedman says the 'diligence and peremptoriness of his rehearsals was sometimes compared with that of Gilbert'.[26] But in 1860 he had only recently come down from Cambridge. His account brings Robson to life for us, with his infuriating waywardness, as well as his charm and genius.[27]

Emden was at his desk in the Manager's office, a ground floor room at the back of the stage, when Burnand arrived. A cheery, rather husky, laugh preceded the entrance of Robson. His head appeared round the door but, seeing Emden had a visitor, he was about to withdraw when Emden sharply recalled him. He shook Burnand's hand heartily, and explained that he had already met Montagu Williams and was sure the piece would be an immense success. Emden drily remarked: 'We'll see!', which immediately deflated Robson. He excused himself and was out of the room and in his brougham in a flash. Emden looked grave, rattled his keys with one hand in his pocket, and held the other out to Burnand. As a special favour he let him out by the back door.

At eleven punctually the next morning the two authors were on stage for the first rehearsal, with four out of the five actors. Robson had not appeared by a quarter to twelve. Emden walked up and down the stage, Mrs. Emden was visibly annoyed and the others shrugged their shoulders.

Horace Wigan, the Stage Director, decided to start without the Lead. Harwood Cooper, as Joe the waiter, was 'discovered sitting at a table, centre, reading about a prize fight in Bell's *Life*'. He read from his part, and the prompter noted down the business in the prompt copy. There was delay over two cues for a bell, and Mrs. Emden's entry as Dorothy had to be fixed. The first five lines of dialogue were gone over about a dozen times, when at the cue 'Who do you think is coming to-day?' there was a commotion at the stage entrance.

In bustled a little figure enveloped in a prodigious ulster, his face partly concealed by a wrapper wound round his neck, and a soft hat pressed down on his forehead. The disguises removed, little Robson was revealed, profuse in apologies, interspersed with novel and humorous explanations and anecdotes, specially introduced for the two authors.

Mrs. Emden signalled to her husband to put a stop to this waste of time. 'Now, Fred, we must get to business!', said Emden. Robson was immediately alert. 'Where were we? Oh, you hadn't come to my part yet? Capital! Of course you're on before me, Horace!' To which Horace Wigan replied in his dry, rather harsh voice: 'Yes, I'm on now.'

Robson then offered a number of suggestions as to business, entries, etc., to Horace Wigan and to Mrs. Stephens. Horace Wigan argued with him, and the matter was submitted to the two authors for arbitration. Emden consulted his watch for the twentieth time in half-an-hour, and called out, 'We can't stop here all day!' to which Robson replied: 'Oh, that'll be all right. We'll pass that now, and fix it tomorrow. Let's get on. Who's next? Who ought to be on?'

To his surprise, he was assured they were waiting for him. He came briskly down stage. 'I beg your pardon, Mr. Robson, but you're heard outside', said the prompter. (To the prompter he was 'Mr. Robson'; to his other colleagues he was 'Fred'.)

'Before I come on?', Robson asked, playing for time. The prompter read the stage directions, and the lines to be heard 'without': 'Right, where's my baggage? Here, waiter, boots, chambermaid, landlady, ostler!'

'I see', said Robson, and went to the back of the stage. On he came downstage again, passing an imaginary window, entering through an imaginary door, calling out for the attendants, until his way was blocked by Joe's table, centre. There was further delay while the position of the table was discussed, Robson giving his views at some length.

Emden interrupted: 'Now get on, get on! We shall never be through the rehearsal at this rate!'

'Quite so!', said Robson, nodding vigorously. 'Now we'll just go back to my entrance!' And he did, but bustled in stage left instead of centre.

'Is that where you've settled to come in, Mr. Robson?', asked the prompter, pencil in hand. 'Yes,' said Robson, annoyed at the interruption. 'We settled it just now.'

'No,' put in Emden gently. 'Excuse me, Fred. You have to come on centre.' The authors agreed, but 'if Mr. Robson saw a better effect . . .

'Oh dear no!', he interrupted blithely. 'I come down centre'.

During further discussion about the position of the table, Mrs. Emden cast her eyes up to the flies, and drew a long breath, and Emden looked at his watch.

Robson begged the prompter not to interrupt him, as although he had only read the play once he was almost letter-perfect. He began his opening speech which was decidedly his own composition, and came to a dead stop, tapped his forehead, stared blankly at the two authors, who had been trying to recognise their own lines, and irritably demanded of the prompter why he did not give him the word. 'Because you told me not to', answered that long-suffering individual, rather sulkily, and told him he had not yet said one word correctly.

Whereupon Robson turned to the two authors, his irritability gone and, chuckling with merriment, told them he had just thought of a first-rate effect for his entrance. (Good Heavens, they were back at his entrance again!) They ran through only four pages of the farce that morning, and everyone was worn-out except Robson.

The next morning he arrived only half-an-hour late, brisk and ready for work. The difficulty was to fix him to any one point. He was immensely amusing, keeping the two authors in spasmodic laughter, and at last getting down to work. The company, word-perfect and weary, was dismissed. Robson remained to go through his soliloquies and business. But he could not be kept at work without an occasional 'refresher'. After a modest 'quencher' the little man was ready to rehearse for hours. Harwood Cooper tells us that Mrs. Emden tried to stop Robson's dresser, Frewin, from going out for 'supplies'. Her own dresser once followed him as far as Farringdon Market in this vain attempt.

Robson made 'an immense hit' in the piece, which ran through the spring into the summer of 1860.

Burnand was to work with Robson on further occasions, and always found him restless at rehearsal, going over and over what dissatisfied him, and bothering his colleagues by changing his business from day to day until he had made up his mind. He was never tired, quick as lightning, and full of energy.[28]

Uncle Zachary and *B.B.* kept the public happy until June 1860, and on 26 June *Shylock* was revived 'for the first time these seven years'. New scenery had been painted by Mr. Telbin 'from sketches taken on the spot', and the 'grosser portions of the burlesque' were either altered or omitted. Frederick Vining now played the Duke, and there was no allusion to the Chief Baron. The 'great artist was putting finishing touches to his portrait'. In the seven years since he had played Shylock he had refined his burlesque style without losing his originality or fire. Experience of straight parts had been an enrichment. The revival was such a success that it ran until 10 September, but it was frequently Robson's only appearance in the evening.

The gentlemanly Frederick Robinson made his first appearance under the new régime on 30 July in *The Scapegoat* and *Somebody Else*, together with Louisa Keeley. *Shylock* wound up the evening.

There had been the usual Holy Week recess, but no summer break was made between the seasons.

5. *Poor Fred!*

The 1860-1861 season began officially on Saturday, 4 August, with little change of programme.

On 17 September Robson went to Birmingham for six nights to play *Hush Money, Medea* ('As performed by express command before Her Majesty and members of the Royal Family'), *Daddy Hardacre* ('enthusiastic reception'), *Uncle Zachary, The Porter's Knot* and *Boots at the Swan.* T. Edgar Pemberton speaks of his 'marvellous impersonation of Samson Burr'.[29]

Back at the Olympic *The Porter's Knot* was revived for three nights only, but was such a draw that its run was continued indefinitely. George Vining played Stephen Scatter for the first time.

A 'new farce' by J. M. Morton was added on 11 October, *A Regular Fix*, recognised by Crabb Robinson as the 30-year-old *Un Coucher de Soleil.* Hugh de Brass (Robson) has fallen asleep in a chair in the house of a respectable solicitor, Mr. Surplus (George Cooke). When he wakes up he cannot remember where he is, nor how he arrived there, and endeavours to find out by cross-questioning the other characters in

. . . a remarkable series of colloquies, which as examples of the perplexed and irrational have never been surpassed. On the colouring of this character Mr. Robson has bestowed the utmost pains, and mere caricature as it is, imparted to it the semblance of nature and consistency . . . one of the richest of his impersonations. (*Times,* 20 October 1860).

This review is one of the most evocative descriptions of his acting in farce. It shows him as a painstaking artist, the creator of a whole gallery of eccentric portraits, each an individual. The farce played for an hour, and except for five minutes Robson was on stage the whole time.

The piece was enthusiastically received, and 'shouts of laughter' proclaimed its success. There could be no greater contrast than that between the pathetic and virtuous Samson Burr and the ridiculous Hugh de Brass, but his public loved him in both. It seems that he could identify happily with either part, once he had nerved himself for the first entry — either by gnawing his arm till it bled, or by a sip of Dutch courage. Once out of the skin of Robson and into that of his allotted

115

character — tragi-comic, sentimental or ridiculous — he was happy, so long as his memory did not desert him. It is a pleasure to dwell on his success in Hugh de Brass, at a time when there were increasing signs of ill-health.

After its 193rd performance on 3 November *The Porter's Knot* was replaced by *Boots at the Swan*.

On Thursday, 29 November, the Olympic was dark: *Daddy Hardacre* and *B.B.* were taken to Windsor, employing nearly the whole company. The theatre was 'arranged' and the scenery painted by W. Grieve, the performance was under the direction of W. B. Donne, and the stage manager was George Ellis.

The Christmas extravaganza was *Timour the Tartar* by John Oxenford and Shirley Brooks, a parody of the once famous melodrama which introduced real horses on to the stage of Drury Lane. The scenery was new, by Mr. Telbin, assisted by Messrs. Gray and Yarnold; machinery by Mr. Sutherland; properties and decorations by Mr. Lightfoot; dresses by Mr. May and Mrs. Renshaw; dances by Mr. Milano; and music arranged by Mr. J. Barnard. Both *The Times* and the *Illustrated London News* praised the scenery.

The outline of the story was kept, but Timour had been transformed from a mere tyrant and bully into a character exploiting Robson's gift for swift transition from rage to absurdity. The dialogue abounded with 'facetious anachronisms' and topical allusions. The leading lady should have been Louisa Pyne, but she was ill, and was replaced by Miss Cotterell who played 'the traditional virago' and sang very well. She and Robson shared the applause at the end. Mrs. Emden, Horace Wigan and George Cooke were commended by *The Times*.

In the Album of Robson's daughter Fanny there is a water-colour of him as Timour (reproduced in plate 4), which gives an impression of frenetic energy; he seems like a man possessed. The costume is certainly 'picturesque'.[30] There seems to have been little subtlety in the interpretation, and the exertion was considerable. Through January and February he played in *Timour* only. *Punch* took him to task for gagging; it seems likely that he forgot his lines. *Timour* was not a great success, in spite of some praise, and ran for 48 performances only.

Hawes T. Craven's 'new and original drama in two acts', *Chimney Corner*, produced on 21 February, was less taxing. One writer called the part of Peter Probity 'the kind in which Mr. Robson particularly shines' — that is, an old man whose honest poverty triumphs over calumny and misfortune. As the cockney owner of a chandler's shop, he has to register simple faith in his son's integrity, then agonies of doubt, then the anguished conviction that his son really has gone off with the cash-box. Westland Marston thought this a Dickensian character, and remembered

his genial self-importance, his delight in his own shrewdness, his occasional mispronunciation of some ambitious passage, uttered with glib enjoyment . . . [31]

During all the action, Grandfather Probity (Horace Wigan), aged 90, sits in the chimney corner, an apparently passive spectator. But in the nick of time he remembers that when everyone was out of the room he had hidden the cash-box in the chimney, and all ends happily. Robson was highly praised, and so was Horace Wigan for his 'delineation of extreme senility', and Mrs. Leigh Murray for her pathetic impersonation of the supposed thief's mother. The part of Peter Probity could not have taxed Robson unduly, yet during its run he appeared in no other play. Queen Victoria saw him for the last time in *Chimney Corner* on 11 March.

On 4 May 1861 (which was the 56th performance) Harwood Cooper's Almanach has the laconic comment 'Poor Fred!', later altered to 'Poor Robson!'. Was this the night, alluded to by several writers, when his memory failed him? According to *The Era* of 12 May 1861, he was taken seriously ill the next morning, Sunday, and did not appear for the rest of the week, his part being played by Horace Wigan. Harwood Cooper confirms this. He was reported to be 'considerably better' on 10 May, Friday, but pleaded 'severe indisposition' as a reason for his absence from the second annual performance in aid of the Royal Dramatic College that night. This indisposition kept him away until 10 June.

This must have been the illness during which Rosetta visited him in Ampthill Square. The death certificate of 12 August 1864 says 'disease of heart and liver two years', which would date back to August 1862, but it seems likely that this serious condition gave warning a year earlier, in the summer of 1861.

To make up for his loss, Miss Amy Sedgewick was advertised to make her first appearance at the Olympic in *The School for Scandal* on 20 May; Mr. Addison was Sir Peter, and Conway the prompter played Robson's old part of Moses. Amy Sedgewick played nightly in *The School* or in *All that Glitters* in the vain hope of compensating patrons for the absence of their hero. But without him 'the deserted house was desolate':

Genius as genius, as distinct from talent and cleverness, is so rare on the English boards that we need not wonder at its being inordinately prized.[32]

On 10 June, 'having recovered from his severe indisposition', Robson appeared in *Ticklish Times,* and received a triumphant welcome from 'a numerous, fashionable and applausive (sic) audience'. He and Miss Sedgewick continued to appear nightly, but in different pieces, except on 29 July when *Plot and Passion* was revived with Miss Sedgewick in Mrs. Stirling's old part. *Poor Pillicoddy* and *The Porter's Knot* were revived in August and on 23 August, the last night, he addressed the audience. He reminded them that the season had lasted nearly two years, and regretted that his sudden and severe illness had kept him away for some weeks of that period, but it was a compensation that the many enquiries after his health had shown him he had even more friends than he had realised. After some facetious allusions to *The Charming Woman* and *The Little Rebel* (roles played by Miss Sedgewick), he took farewell of the audience until 23 September. The partners appeared together, and the evening closed with *Catching an Heiress* and 'The Song of the Country Fair'.

6. *Last Appearances at the Olympic, and Lost Opportunities*

The Public was respectfully informed that the theatre would be open for the season on Monday, 23 September, and that Mr. Robson would appear every evening. On the first night *Married Daughters* employed most of the company, and Robson followed with *Poor Pillicoddy* and *Catching an Heiress*. But a week later he was again 'indisposed', and did not return until 28 October.

At this point Emden wisely engaged Henry Neville; not another Robson, but a strikingly handsome young actor of a very different type, who was to make a big name for himself and save the theatre when Robson's career was over. He made his first appearance at the Olympic on Thursday, 3 October 1861, in *Jack of all Trades.*

Robson returned in John Oxenford's *A Legal Impediment* on 28 October. He played a stuttering, bemused lawyer's clerk, mistaken for a romantic lover in disguise, who is involved in all kinds of false situations. A moment much appreciated by the audience was when he first tried an olive: 'They looks like gooseberries, and they tastes like periwinkles.' The audience received him back with enthusiasm and, moved by their applause, he murmured a quiet 'God bless you!'.

A Blighted Being was revived on 9 December, and he seemed to be getting back to his old form. But on 11 December he wrote to Emden asking to be excused rehearsal as he was 'in such a stage of influenza, cough, cold and sore throat'. He hoped Emden himself was better, so this illness was probably a seasonal one.

Deerfoot on 16 December was an attempt by Francis Burnand to do something on the lines of *B.B.* The hero is mistaken for a Red Indian backed to win a foot-race. Burnand probably thought the formula was bound to succeed, but *Deerfoot* ran only a week.

But the Boxing Day extravaganza, *The King of the Merrows,* was 'just suited to Mr. Robson'. It was founded on a fairy tale by F. Palgrave Simpson and laid in 'primitive Ireland'. Dan the Piper (Robson) feigns idiocy and plays upon enchanted pipes; this throws the sea into commotion, and enables him to visit the dominion of Coomora, King of the Merrows. Dan's piping makes the king dance until he falls asleep, enabling the captive Prince to escape with his true love, Sabrina, to the world above. When Coomora wakes he turns Dan into a sea monster, but the fairy queen turns him back to his own shape, and the lovers are made happy. The 'pretty story' was provided with 'magnificent scenery' by Mr. Telbin. The submarine palace and the concluding scene were particularly admired. The dialogue was 'seasoned with puns and parodies', and Robson had a medley song called 'An Epitome of Home and Foreign News'. The 'elegant fairy story' ran for 51 nights, not long by extravaganza standards.

Robson's next new part was another sentimental old gentleman — Abel Milford in *Fairy's Father* by C. S. Cheltnam — on 24 February. Abel is the property man in the theatre where his daughter performs as a fairy. He is preparing a feast of rabbit and onions to celebrate her eighteenth birthday. When she brings a young man home with her, he is alarmed, and, to test the young man's integrity, recounts how he himself was once wrongly suspected of fraud and had to leave home and change his name. The young man reveals that his own father had confessed on his deathbed to the crime of which Abel was wrongly accused. All ends happily:

> Mr. Robson has in this part one which brings out his best qualities, and a more interesting domestic piece has seldom been placed upon the stage.

By 'best qualities' the writer clearly meant those most likely to edify, and by a 'domestic piece' one with a good moral tone. The first night drew a full house, and *Fairy's Father* was followed by the absurdities of *Retained for the Defence,* in which Robson's Pawkins was supported by Henry Neville's Mr. Whitewash.

The two pieces kept Robson's public happy for eight weeks, and might have continued for longer if the approach of Easter had not prompted the management to produce a new extravaganza — Francis Burnand's *Fair Rosamund.* The story of *Fair Rosamund* was popular about this

time with the Pre-Raphaelites. The bower at Woodstock and the Here-
fordshire countryside gave scope to Messrs. Telbin and Grieve, Mr.
G. Cooke was much admired as Sir Trusty, Horace Wigan uttered
French puns with relish, and Miss Cotterell was a gallant figure as
Henry II with a tunic at least four inches above her knees. But,
although Robson's Queen Eleanor was 'irresistibly funny', it was not
one of his best parts. He rode upon a rocking-horse in a costume and
coiffure more reminiscent of Queen Victoria than Queen Eleanor. If
we exclude such brief appearances as Signora Dumplino in *A Day after
the Fair* and the ballad-seller disguise in *The Discreet Princess*, Medea
was his only successful dame part at the Olympic. He stayed the
course in *Fair Rosamund* for two months, but played nothing else the
same evening. According to Harwood Cooper he was 'ill' on at least
one occasion, when Warboys played his part.

After the 60th and last performance of *Fair Rosamund* on 28 April he
disappeared for two weeks. It was announced that he would shortly
re-appear in *The Porter's Knot*, which he did on 7 July.

There was no summer break, and Robson continued to play his most
popular characters in *Boots at the Swan*, *To Oblige Benson* and *The
Porter's Knot* until the end of September. After a week of *Daddy
Hardacre* he took his 'annual congé', with the promise of appearing in
'a new drama'. Henry Neville and Amy Sedgewick appeared regularly
in *The Dowager*, but during Robson's 'congé' Kate Saville (Helen
Faucit's niece) replaced Amy Sedgewick as leading lady.

When Robson returned it was in *The Wandering Minstrel* only. In
All that Glitters, *Real and Ideal*, etc., the company was led by one or
both of the potential stars, Kate Saville and Henry Neville. Because of
the success of *The Wandering Minstrel* the 'new drama' had to be
postponed.

But on Monday, 10 November 1862, Watts Phillips' *Camilla's Husband* (originally called *Married in Haste*) finally appeared. Kate Saville
and Henry Neville played the hero and heroine supported by a large
cast, which included Robson as Dogbriar, the wandering tinker who is
responsible for the final unravelling of a far-fetched plot.

As Marston says, the part on paper seems commonplace, and the
tinker's love of high-sounding words (*feel*osophy, *mo*rality,
*need*cessity, etc.) with occasional malapropisms makes the dialogue
tedious. Yet:

. . . there was an air of conviction, a tone of sincerity and consistency in Robson's acting that seemed to make the tinker a
philosopher in his way . . . That the piece succeeded was chiefly due

to Robson's skill in creating a character from the slightest hints, to the vigour and romance which Mr. Henry Neville threw into the part of the hero.[33]

The author dedicated the published play to Henry Neville, whose 'high histrionic talents' seemed to him to be the chief factor in its success.

Others thought less well of Robson than did Marston. Perhaps Marston was lucky enough to see him on a 'good' night, but during the run of *Camilla's Husband* there were, alas, many nights that were very bad indeed. Clement Scott wrote:

> I saw him last in Watts Phillips' play 'Camilla's Husband' as a travelling tinker who came on with a donkey. But Robson was a wreck of his former self. His memory had gone, his power vanished, he was incoherent with his words and business. He was Robson the genius no more!

He played in nothing else except for a week of *The Wandering Minstrel*, and a special performance in *Boots*, in aid of the Lancashire Relief Fund on 17 December 1862 at the Princess's, under the patronage of the Lord Mayor. Robson and Mrs. Selby were the only professionals. Frank Archer, one of his greatest admirers, was there. He thought him the greatest actor he had ever seen, and did not consider the word genius as applied to him at all exaggerated. He thought it 'a great thing' to speak to him, and hung about the entrances hoping to do so. There is therefore no malice in his description of the dresser 'following Robson about with a tumbler which it was painful to see he clutched at nervously', gulping down the contents before making his entrance. He exaggerated, and indulged 'in antics beyond all reason', once on the stage.[35]

There was no part for Robson in the Christmas extravaganza, Burnand's *Robin Hood*.

Sir William Hardman recalls a visit to the Olympic in February of the following year to see *Camilla's Husband*, when the Prince of Wales was in the Royal Box:

> The performance was execrably bad, Robson, who had a drunken part specially written for him (a tinker gipsy in a chronic state of booze) was actually so screwy that he could scarcely act.[36]

A white satin playbill for 7 February 1863, indicating a Royal visit, is preserved among the papers left by E. M. Robson. He must have been about eight years old at the time, and had probably recently joined the family at 19 Ampthill Square. In later life he was a circumspect, quiet, domestic character and did not mix much with his fellow professionals.

He probably acquired an early horror of 'conviviality' from what he had seen of its effect upon his 'Uncle'.

A few days later, Crabb Robinson saw *Camilla's Husband* and reported:'The charm of Robson's acting is gone; he takes to drinking.'

Harwood Cooper traces his mental and physical decline. He claims as the first symptom in.1860 a weakness of voice when Robson went on from the Olympic, 'dressed and in a cab', to perform *B.B.* at the Royal Italian Opera House in aid of the funds of the Royal Dramatic College. *B.B.* was preceded by scenes from *Money, The Merchant of Venice, Macbeth, The School for Scandal* and *Black-eyed Susan* (in which the veteran T. P. Cooke returned to dance his hornpipe, and J. L. Toole appeared as Gnatbrain). There was singing by Catherine Hayes, Louisa Pyne and Harrison, a selection by the Christy Minstrels, and *Box and Cox,* played by Buckstone and Compton.

The theatre was so full that Emden had to go up into the Gallery, and complained: 'I couldn't hear you, Robson.' Did he really suffer from a serious throat complaint, such as laryngeal consumption or cancer, as some obituary writers alleged? We know there was a throat weakness, but it must be remembered that the theatre was much larger than that in which he was used to perform, and that he probably had no rehearsal. Even more serious:

Rehearsals called for Daddy Grey Deaf Hero.* Robson's memory fails him. Rehearsal dismissed. Emden tells me he will be ruined. Robson's salary stopped, £40 per week. Wandering Minstrel. What's next Cooper?

This may allude to an announcement on 8 September that numerous applications had been received for *Daddy Hardacre, Boots at the Swan* and *The Wandering Minstrel.* The last two were revived in December 1862, but not *Daddy Hardacre.* The £40 was probably a fine. Finally:

Robson drinks . . . loses his memory . . . kills himself with drink mind becomes affected.

Harwood Cooper may be guilty of occasional inaccuracy, but over-all his account of Robson's decline is convincing. He says nothing of any disease of the throat or larynx, although he does recall an instance in which Conway the prompter rebuked him for forcing his voice, and warned him he might do himself permanent damage if he persisted. Drink, affecting the liver and the mind, was the cause of death according to Harwood Cooper, confirmed by the death certificate. The loss of memory alluded to in *The Era* of 3 October 1869 implies that it was not

---

*This presumably means *Daddy Hardacre* and *Boots at the Swan.*

122

only at rehearsal that he had black-outs, but also in at least one performance, which many playgoers would recall.

Although our main concern is the gradual and sad disintegration of Robson's powers, we should spare a thought for his fellow lessee and his colleagues. Almost to the end, in spite of his many lapses, Robson remained the chief asset of the Olympic, and while there was a possibility of his performing his audiences clamoured for him. He could never be relied on, nor could he be dispensed with — that was Emden's dilemma.

In addition to his uncertainty about Robson, Emden was suffering like all managers from the depression in the cotton industry, caused by the American Civil War. He also had worries in connection with the lease of the theatre, in particular doubts as to the *bona fides* of the sleeping partner, G. C. Bentinck, M.P. Apparently Bentinck had neglected to renew the seven-year lease, and was proposing to form a Limited Liability Company, of which he and Tom Taylor would be Directors, with Emden to 'superintend the Treasury'. Emden was to have some shares, but not Robson. Bentinck had probably little faith in Robson's future drawing-power or business ability.

Yet during those uneasy months from the winter of 1862 to the spring of 1863, when he seemed capable of little but stumbling through Dogbriar, three writers at least had enough faith in him to write 'Robson parts'.

The first to come to mind is Melter Moss in Tom Taylor's *The Ticket-of-leave Man*. Thieves' agent and informer, Melter Moss is a short part, and he does not appear at all in the second act. But Robson in his prime could have made him important, as he made Desmarets important. *The Ticket-of-leave Man* is generally considered a landmark in nineteenth-century drama, one of the first attempts at social realism on the stage. It was certainly stronger and more original than most of the Olympic repertoire, though it was also based on a French original (*Le Retour de Melun*). In the event, the part written for Robson was played by G. Vincent, who made of it 'a most extravagant affair' and played to the audience. Hawkshaw, the detective, was the first solid success of Horace Wigan, and Bob Brierly, the Ticket-of-leave Man who proves his innocence, was a triumph for Henry Neville.

Harwood Cooper speaks of *The Ticket-of-leave Man* as Robson's 'death-blow', meaning that to be banished from the Olympic while the rising star, Henry Neville, saved the fortunes of the theatre was the ultimate humiliation. But he adds that Robson had 'luck to the end', since as joint lessee and manager he shared in the profits.

Hawes Craven wrote for Robson the part of Daniel the Milkman in *Milky White*. Daniel is very deaf and very litigious. His deafness is cured by the shock of hearing his daughter wish for the money she was to inherit at his death. The plot is fairly silly, but he would undoubtedly have had a facile success. Harwood Cooper is mistaken in saying that James Rogers made a success of it at 'the merry little Strand'. James Rogers died suddenly on 14 April 1863, at the height of his powers, ten days after Robson's last appearance at the Olympic. It was the author himself who played it from 26 September 1864 until the following April, after Robson's death.

In a personal letter kept by Robson's daughter Fanny, Charles Reade writes under the date 12 March (but with no year):

> I have received a line from the theatre telling me you have got *It is never too late to mend*, and that Isaac Levi is the part you are sweet upon. Isaac ought to feel very much flattered . . . but viewed as a character I consider him a mere conventional production, and should never have thought of proposing him to you.
>
> Crawley and Jack I look upon as characters, and hope a perusal of the ms. may lead you to the same conclusion.
>
> But we will have a talk over it at the Theatre some night; for I'll be bound you have something in your head that has not occurred to me.[37]

Reade's sensational and propagandist novel, *It is Never Too Late to Mend*, was itself based on his play *Gold*, produced at Drury Lane on 10 January 1853. Australian gold-mines were much in the news at that time. (Mrs. Alfred Phillips' *Life in Australia* at the Olympic in the spring of 1853 will be recalled.) In the early 1860s Reade planned to make a new and better play from the novel. Malcolm Elwin says Reade was occupied in this work 'during 1864'. 1863 would seem a likely year for the letter to Robson, although 1864 is not impossible.[38]

The story is of a young farmer who emigrates to Australia in order to earn the £1,000 required by his sweetheart's father as a condition of their marriage. He goes through many vicissitudes among the 'savages', as a sheep-farmer and a gold-digger. There is a sub-plot with a sensational 'exposure' of the brutalities of the English penal system. The character Robson was 'sweet upon' was Levi; he appears first as a sentimental old gentleman pleading not to be evicted from his house: 'Let me rest in my little tent until I rest for ever . . .'. He then turns upon his persecutors: 'I spit on ye! I curse ye!'. In the last act he is able to bring about the happy ending by spying upon a robbery. It was a short part, which Boucicault had advised Reade to cut out, but it was certainly of a Robsonian type and would have been another Jewish study to add to Moses, Shylock and Reuben. When the play was produced at the Princess's the year after Robson's death, 'the refined habitués' objected to the dismal details of the prison scenes. It was described as 'an interesting drama of modern social life', and for all its melodrama was a forerunner of a new kind of stage realism — like *The Ticket-of-leave Man.*

A fourth lost opportunity was the character of the Deal pilot, a kind of Peggotty, in Francis Burnand's *The Deal Boatman.* Burnand left the manuscript of the first Act for Robson to look over, and two nights later went to see him at the theatre:

> . . . while he was dressing for the part he was then playing, he commenced off-hand rehearsing the new piece . . . he was 'called' and hurried from his dressing-room upstairs down on to the stage.

When his scene was over he returned to rehearsing the new piece, suggesting business, etc. Burnand stayed chatting with him in the wings, until the last scene claimed him; he shook Burnand's hand heartily, went on the stage and it seems that this was the last Burnand saw of him.

The next day he was taken seriously ill, a severe and unexpected relapse, described as a 'stroke'. Burnand telescopes events, saying that 'shortly afterwards he died'. Even if that were his last performance at the Olympic, he still had a year and five months to live, and out of that time about a year of acting in the provinces. Burnand does not tell us the name of the play in which Robson was acting with so little involvement that he could rehearse another in his brief moments off-stage. *The Deal Boatman* appeared at Drury Lane on 21 September 1863, when Robson was still alive, with Belmore in 'his' part. Belmore was described by Clement Scott as one of the only three actors of power to succeed Robson.[39]

That such opportunities were still offered him by playwrights in his last year or two shows that he was not always ill or drink-sodden. There was enough of the old Robson left to inspire respect in these writers. Clearly, he varied a great deal. Burnand says 'he would be seriously ill', would recover, and then be himself again. Burnand's picture of the last time he saw him shows a man still able to be enthusiastic over a new part, still showing some of his old zest.

After the 92nd and last performance of *Camilla's Husband, The Lottery Ticket* was revived for Robson 'by desire', and he seems to have performed this nightly from 2-24 March, the rest of the bill being provided by his colleagues. On Tuesday, 10 March, all theatres were open free, by command of the Prince of Wales, in honour of his marriage. After *The Lottery Ticket* the National Anthem was sung.

On 23 March *Ticklish Times* was substituted for *The Lottery Ticket*, and continued until Easter with the exception of Good Friday. On Easter Saturday, 4 April, just over ten years since his first appearance there, Robson performed for the last time at the Olympic in *Ticklish Times*.

There was no announcement. Did he have another collapse? Or were his appearances becoming such an embarrassment to himself, the management, and the public that he was allowed to fade quietly away?

It is pleasanter to think that it was on Easter Saturday, in the intervals of *Ticklish Times,* that he and Burnand discussed *The Deal Boatman,* and that on this last night he was in such good form. If so, the sudden collapse must have been on Easter Sunday.

7. *Exile from the Olympic, and Last Illness*

It was six or seven weeks before he acted again, and then he went to the Prince of Wales's at Liverpool, an engagement which may have been planned in advance. Young Fred called these seasons out of London 'starring tours', but Harwood Cooper summed them up as visiting 'occasionally the country towns with some of his characters'. Harwood Cooper was playing Maltby in *The Ticket-of-leave Man* and may have been understandably contemptuous of provincial playhouses.

According to Young Fred, Mr. Snell the lawyer said that Robson (being in poor health) should make his Will, and took the draft to Liverpool. But the Will was signed on 18 May, and the Liverpool engagement began on 25 May, so perhaps the so-called draft was a copy.

Young Fred was at that time in the Liverpool company, and played Smoothly Quirk to his father's Samson Burr in *The Porter's Knot*. When Samson Burr had to say: 'I've seen that face before!' there was a roar of laughter. Young Fred was said to bear a striking resemblance to his father. His pictures (e.g. in Burnand's *Ulysses)* show a longer, leaner face, but there must have been some resemblance in manner, gait or voice, since the likeness is commented on by many writers. Of Samson Burr, the press wrote:

> The sly, twinkling badinage of the first scene was in wonderful opposition with the terrible life-weariness of that in which the poor old porter is reduced again to bitter labour, quite beyond his failing strength.

Besides *The Porter's Knot, Boots at the Adelphi* (so called to please the local audience) was played in the first week:

> . . . in detail wonderfully natural. Mr. Robson easily convulses an audience in this part by the mere twitching of nose or eyebrow . . .

There were 'magnificent houses' and enthusiastic audiences. Even allowing for the possibly lower standards of Liverpool, it seems that he was in better health than during the last weeks at the Olympic.

The second week brought another contrast: Daddy Hardacre and Lancelot Griggs. His performances earned 'the just reward which such masterly and perfect impersonations alone could meet with'. At his Benefit 'he seldom if ever played better', and to 'a demonstrative and appreciative audience'.

From Liverpool father and son (and probably the rest of the family) moved to the Queen's Theatre, Dublin, opening on 15 June for a fortnight. They 'drew exceedingly good houses' for *The Porter's Knot, The Wandering Minstrel, Pawkins the Persecuted* (i.e. *Retained for the Defence*), *Daddy Hardacre, Ticklish Times, Hush Money* and *The Lottery Ticket,* sharing the bill with ballet. 'Warm, enthusiastic applause' was bestowed on all his characters; his popularity seemed to have increased by his prolonged absence'. Young Fred's début was greeted with such applause as to add 'an additional spark of pleasure to his father's eye'. 'Genuine pride and pleasure lit up old Robson's expressive little face.' (Old? He was 41.) The engagement was prolonged until 4 July, and when called before the curtain on the last night Mr. Robson said he meant to return to Dublin soon, an announcement which was greeted with great applause.

He opened on Monday, 6 July, in *The Porter's Knot* and *Boots at the Swan* at the Theatre Royal, Birmingham to a thin and somewhat restless audience. The *Birmingham Daily Post* considered that a diet of tawdry melodrama had made the public unable to appreciate the natural, refined and unaffected acting of the most popular and gifted English actor of the day. The critic admitted that in voice and physical power Mr. Robson was weaker than of old, but in artistic conception, thorough consistency and a wonderful blending of humour and pathos, there was no mistaking the impress of genius. As an instance of his humour, the critic quoted the old porter's account of his early privations: 'Dumpling after dumpling, and no apple at all — it's rather dull work, believe me!'; and of his pathos, the scene in which Samson Burr and his wife sit side by side on the barrow, talking of the past. Young Fred as Smoothly Quirk was well received, but still had much to learn. The critic considered it would be a waste of time to review an impersonation so well known as that of *Boots at the Swan*. (Clearly, time or space had run out). *The Era* also admitted that Robson's voice was weaker than it used to be, but judged his acting as fine and comic as ever.

On 27 July Henry Webb of the Queen's Theatre, Dublin, 'broke the slumber' of the Theatre Royal, Belfast, for six nights, and 'regaled his northern country men' with a theatrical treat. Unlike Birmingham, the theatre was crowded and gave Robson 'a heartily Irish welcome', when he made his first entry in *The Porter's Knot*, and they were not disappointed. 'One is led to believe they are looking on reality, not acting,' said *The Era* somewhat inelegantly.

'Twelve nights of unclouded prosperity' were 'wafted' over the theatre, and the audience enjoyed the same Robsonian fare as had been offered at Birmingham, with the important addition of *Medea*.

On 31 July 1863 *Medea* marked the first appearance on any stage of the eight-year-old Edwin May Robson, billed as 'Master Robson' in the part of Lycaon. Fanny Robson wrote out the part for him, and a manuscript note in a playbill preserved by his daughter says that Creusa was played by 'Mrs. F. Robson', under the name of 'Miss Hastings'.[40] Was this an isolated appearance, because someone was ill, or because she wanted to keep a close eye on her husband? It is possible that she had been acting off and on in a small way through the years of separation while she was rearing Edwin. Rosetta remains something of a mystery. Her Declaration (see Appendix 2: The Paternity of E. M. Robson) does not ring true, and her grand-children (Fanny's children) thought her so disagreeable that they ran away crying to the nursery when she came to the house. But Edwin wrote to her with great affection, and she had one remarkable gift: she was so good with baby animals that the Zoo keepers allowed her behind the scenes to handle them.[41]

Liverpool, Dublin, Birmingham and Belfast could have been called a 'starring tour', but on 6 September we read in *The Era* an appeal to Provincial Managers by Butler and Danvers, agents, on behalf of Mr. Robson, the Celebrated Comedian: that Robson should be cadging for provincial dates seems a sad state of affairs. Whatever came of their efforts, Butler and Danvers do not seem to have remained his agents for long, since on 12 October Mr. Richard Thorne (Lessee of the Theatre Royal, Margate) presented his 'already powerful dramatic corps' at the Theatre Royal, Canterbury, with the Great Comedian, Mr. F. Robson. For two weeks Robson topped the bill with *The Porter's Knot*, *Boots at the Swan*, *Daddy Hardacre*, *Medea* and *Pawkins*, with the powerful dramatic corps playing *Lady Audley's Secret*, *The Spoiled*

Child and *Rob the Rip* as well as providing some principal danseuses. 'Miss Hastings' was in the company, playing Creusa again, and Esther in *Daddy Hardacre*.

On 26 October Robson was back in Edinburgh, for the first time for five years, playing to 'a warm reception' in a well-filled house. There were 'too frequent signs of feebleness', but his powers of pathos still made him 'superior to any living actor'.

On 6 December Richard Thorne was advertising for supporting actors for Mr. F. Robson's tour, starting at Canterbury, and on Boxing Day Mr. Thorne's 'talented dramatic company' and Mr. Robson opened at the Theatre Royal, Canterbury. Once more he was supported by his wife as Esther, and also as Julia in *The Wandering Minstrel*, Mrs. Benson in *To Oblige Benson,* and Agatha de Windsor in *Pawkins*. She also joined the 'talented company' as Maria in *The Spoiled Child* and Wilhelmina in *The Waterman*. Not satisfied with the talent, Richard Thorne advertised again for actors and actresses to join Mr. Robson's tour at Margate on 1 February. He also advertised for theatres willing to engage the company and its star.

They seem to have been at Margate for a week, where Robson played 'most of his favourite characters', and in the course of the spring were at Wolverhampton, Newcastle-under-Lyme and Coventry, all rather third-rate. At Coventry Rosetta discarded her alias and was described as 'Mrs. Robson'. According to *The Era* of 21 February 1864 Robson received a perfect ovation after *The Porter's Knot,* although the audience was not large. But by the last night (19 February) the house was full for *Ticklish Times* and *Pawkins,* after which Robson made 'a neat speech', hoping to return.

He was back in Edinburgh from 22 March to 4 April, independently, and supported by the stock company as usual. However, the audience was 'unkind to him, mistaking his infirmity'. His Benefit was under the patronage of HRH Prince Alfred. This was followed by a brief and disastrous engagement at Stoke, where his terrible cough was more audible than his words.

There were probably other small engagements, but enough has been said to show that Frederick Robson was a worn-out man, with only the tattered remains of his art left. Back home, he had the conviction that

. . . he should never tread the Olympic stage again and throughout his last illness he is said to have wailed, 'Oh my wasted and unprofitable life!'.[42]

It was not admitted to the press that the illness was mortal, and there was even a report that he might be well enough to appear at the Olympic before the end of the season. Indeed, he was described as 'ill, but recovering'.[43]

By the end of June he was clearly very ill, and a second opinion was called in. William Fergusson, a distinguished surgeon, wrote to Mrs. Robson saying he would meet Dr. Andrews at 19 Ampthill Square on 28 June at 6 o'clock.[44] 'Surgeon' in the nineteenth century did not necessarily mean one who performed surgical operations, but Fergusson was so qualified, and may have been called in to advise on the possibility of operation in the case of throat cancer. On the other hand, Fergusson had many friends in the acting profession, and was probably a personal friend, so that the visit and consultation with Dr. Andrews might have been just an act of friendship towards the patient and his wife. About this time dropsy set in, and Dr. Andrews had already given him up.[45]

The end came on 12 August. The cause of death given in the death certificate by Dr. Andrews was: Disease of Heart and Liver two years; Dropsy six weeks.

Young Fred was in Dublin at the time, having some success in his father's old part of Wormwood and as Azucena in a burlesque of *Il Trovatore*.

The obituaries were numerous, the best being *The Times, The Era* and *Tallis's*. Several bad poems also appeared. *The Era* of 21 August said that Mr. Robson's death was received with great regret in his native town, where he had appeared the previous season (probably the first week in February, before Newcastle-under-Lyme and Coventry).

On the day of the funeral, Thursday, 18 August, the Olympic Theatre was closed as a mark of respect. Although he had not acted there for over a year, his name had remained as joint lessee and manager with Emden. Not only the actors but the entire staff of the Olympic seem to have been at Norwood Cemetery — the money and check takers, the carpenters, the property men, and even the old woman who sold fruit outside the theatre, with whom he used to joke when he went in and out. His dresser, Mr. Frewin, 'seemed much affected'. There were many other members of the theatrical profession, including his old friend J. L. Toole, and George Belmore, who played the *Deal Boatman* part written by Burnand for Robson.

Three mourning coaches followed the hearse to Norwood, a journey which took four and a half hours. Why the long journey? Presumably because the Brookes family had a plot in the Norwood cemetery. In the coaches were Robson's mother, Margaret Brownbill, who lived until 1879 in South London; his widow; his son and daughter, and his 'nephew of whom he was very fond'; his friends, Dr. and Mrs.

Brookes; his lawyer, his doctor, and Mr. and Mrs. Emden. According to *The Era* the Chaplain read 'the usual lessons rather inaudibly', which did not prevent those present from being 'visibly affected'.

In course of time an impressive monument was erected, a Portland stone column on bases, but by 1971 this had collapsed and the inscription was illegible. It was difficult to find the fragments among the long grass and brambles. Now that part of the cemetery has been levelled, and Robson is commemorated by a simple marker with name, dates and the one word

ACTOR.

NOTES TO PART III

[1] *The Entr'acte Annual*, London 1893.

[2] John Hollingshead: *My Lifetime*, London 1895.

[3] Tom Taylor: 'Phelps and the Fool's Revenge', *The Theatre*, new series, London, 1 December 1878.

[4] See (1) and (2) above.

[5] Elliott O'Donnell: *Great Thames Mysteries*, London 1929.

[6] Quoted in Roger Fulford: *Dearest Child*, London 1964.

[7] See also George Rowell: *Queen Victoria goes to the Theatre*, London 1978.

[8] Kenneth Robinson: *Wilkie Collins*, 2nd Edition, London 1975.

[9] *Ibid.*

[10] J. L. Toole: *J. L. Toole, Chronicled by himself*, London 1892.

[11] E. L. Blanchard: *Life and Reminiscences*, edited by Clement Scott and Cecil Howard, London 1912.

[12] H. Crabb Robinson: *The London Theatre 1811-1866*, edited by Eiluned Brown, London, STR, 1966.

[13] Westland Marston: *Our Recent Actors*, Vol. II, London 1888.

[14] H. Barton Baker: *History of the London Stage*, London 1904.

[15] Clement Scott: *The Drama Yesterday and To-Day*, London 1889.

[16] *Ibid.*

[17] See (12) above.

[18] Squire Bancroft: *Recollections of 60 Years,* London 1909.

[19] See (11) above.

[20] See (10) above.

[21] In the possession of Mrs. José Smith, great-grand-daughter of Frederick Robson and C. B. Brookes.

[22] Family tradition.

[23] See Appendix 2: The Paternity of E. M. Robson.

[24] *Ibid.*

[25] See (18) above.

[26] Dr. Jane W. Stedman: 'General Utility; Victorian Author Actors from Knowles to Pinero', *Educational Theatre*, October 1972.

[27] Francis Burnand: 'A Genius Nearly Forgotten', *Britannia*, London, October 1907.

[28] J. Brander Mathews and Laurence Hutton: *Actors and Actresses of Great Britain and the U.S.*, London 1886.

[29] T. Edgar Pemberton: *The Theatre Royal Birmingham*, Birmingham 1888.

[30] In 1976 the Album was in the possession of Miss Kathleen Gent, who gave me permission to have the sketch photographed. Since her death it has disappeared.

[31] See (13) above.

[32] Unidentified cutting.

[33] See (13) above.

[34] See (15) above.

[35] Frank Archer: *An Actor's Notebook*, London 1912.

[36] S. M. Ellis (ed.): *A Mid-Victorian Pepys* (Letters and Memoirs of Sir William Hardman), London 1923.

[37] Kindly shown to me by the late Miss Kathleen Gent.

[38] Malcolm Elwin: *Charles Reade*, London 1931.

[39] See (15) above.

[40] Kindly shown to me by Mr. Edward Fottrell.

[41] Family tradition.

[42] *Kentish Observer*, 25 August 1864.

[43] *Tallis's*, 13 August 1864.

[44] Kindly shown to me by the late Miss Kathleen Gent.

[45] G. A. Sala: *Frederick Robson*, London 1864.

Appendix I

The Descendants of Frederick Robson

Robson's daughter Frances ('Fanny') married Robert Charles Brookes, surgeon, eldest son of Charles Brookes, Robson's friend 'C.B.' (also a surgeon) in 1871. They were members of a family of doctors long connected with Lambeth. Robert Charles and his brothers, Walter and Frederick, had a surgery in the Westminster Bridge Road, near the Canterbury Music Hall, and among their patients were Louis Wain and Dan Leno. Fanny and Robert Charles Brookes had eight children. The eldest, Frederick Charles (named after his two grandfathers), died in infancy and was buried in Frederick Robson's grave at Norwood. Kathleen Gent, daughter of Maude, the fourth child, and Mrs. José Smith, daughter of Sydney, the seventh, are frequently mentioned in the text. I am grateful to them for passing on family reminiscences, and for showing me the Mazeppa cane, the Yellow Dwarf cigar case, and other Robsoniana, as well as pictures. Mrs. José Smith has two sons, Robert and Richard, Frederick Robson's great-great-grandsons. Kathleen Gent died from a tragic accident in 1977.

Robson's son, Frederick Henry, made a good start on the stage, as mentioned in the text. His likeness to his father was commented on, particularly in Burnand's *Ulysses*, but is not apparent in photographs; there young Fred has a longer, leaner face than his father's, and seems to be taller, although I have no record of his height. He popped up here and there in playbills in different parts of the country and sometimes played his father's old characters — such as Mr. Trotter Southdown (at the Charing Cross in 1869). He married Emelie Eyre Jones, aged nineteen, on 11 May 1870, and there is therefore a strong presumption that a Miss Eyre Robson acting in the 1890s was their daughter. There may have been other children. He wrote plays: *The Varsity Boat Race* (with C. H. Stephenson), produced at The Lyceum on 6 April 1870; *Popacatapetl*, Holborn, 18 December 1872; *Lady Godiva*, Middlesbrough, 5 May 1873; and *How to kill him*, Stockton-on-Tees, 14 July 1873. But he seems to have disappeared from the family tradition, since neither Mrs. José Smith nor Miss Kathleen Gent had ever heard their grandmother had a brother, though they knew E. M. Robson as 'Uncle Edwin', in spite of his dubious right to that title.

At the time of E. M. Robson's claim to be the Great Fred's son in 1895 (see

133

Appendix 2) when young Fred wrote to the press, the *Manchester Umpire* commented that ' . . . he seemed to have gone under . . . but used to advertise for engagements'. Perhaps someone reading this book may know something more of the mystery surrounding his later years. In 1919 he died in Lambeth, aged 75, described as 'formerly an actor', survived by his wife. The death was certified by Frederick Brookes, M.R.C.S., brother of Robert Charles, Fanny's husband.

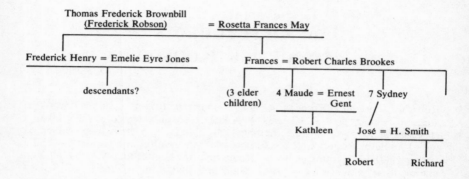

Appendix II

The Paternity of Edwin May Robson

Edwin May Robson's first appearance on any stage was as one of Medea's children at Belfast (see above). He became a very competent actor, sought-after for small but important character parts. On tour with Jerrold Robertshaw he played in everything from Shakespeare to Ibsen; landmarks were *Saints and Sinners* and *Trelawney of the Wells*. (He called his house at Chiswick 'Trelawney'.) During the early years of the twentieth century there was scarcely an All Star matinée without E. M. Robson in a minor yet essential role. His Fluellen was particularly commended. He also wrote plays: *Faithful unto Death* (in collaboration with E. Compton), produced at Bristol in 1881, and *The Foundling*, produced at Terry's in 1894. A pile of manuscript plays was found among his effects after his death.

He was a quiet, domestic character, devoted to his 'dearest mother', Mrs. Rosetta Robson, and his wife Elizabeth Almahide Smith, whom he married in 1879. According to an old friend, Mrs. Yukins, interviewed by the writer in 1975, he was prouder of his work for anti-vivisection than for any theatrical achievements, and he hated anything 'common'.

Until his marriage he was known as a nephew of the great Robson, to whom he bore little resemblance except short stature and carotty hair. But on the day before the wedding, 8 December 1879, Mrs. Rosetta Brownbill made a Declaration to the effect that he was her son and the son of Frederick Robson. This Declaration was not then published in the press, and was presumably made for the sake of the bride and her parents. In the marriage register Edwin May Robson is described as son of the late Frederick Robson.

Nothing more was heard of the matter until 1895, when E. M. Robson went to Balmoral with Mr. and Mrs. Alexander's company to act in *Liberty Hall*. Queen Victoria congratulated him on his performance, and recalled having seen 'his father' in her younger days.

This was reported in the press, and provoked a letter from Frederick Robson the younger, saying that he was his father's only son, and that E. M. Robson was a nephew of his mother's. Possibly urged by his wife's relatives to whom his legitimacy meant much, E. M. Robson now came out into the open and sent the 1879 Declaration to the press. It was published in *The People* on 6 October, and copied or commented on in other papers. From then onwards he described himself as 'son' when occasion arose.

Frederick Robson the younger, Robert Charles Brookes (now married to Fanny Robson) and Maria Bailey the housemaid at Ampthill Square then made

Declarations that E. M. Robson was not and could not be the son of the Great Robson (see Declarations 1, 2 and 3). It seems that these declarations were not published, but were sent with a covering note from Walter John Brookes, Robson's executor, to Messrs. Gatti.

Copies were found among the papers of E. M. Robson inherited by Mr. Edward Fottrell, a cousin on Mrs. E. M. Robson's side, at the death of their only daughter, Rosetta or Rosie. E. M. Robson died in 1932. There was also theatrical material of great interest, already quoted in the text, and which Mr. Fottrell kindly made available to me.

Declaration 1

Declaration of Mrs. R. F. Brownbill known as Mrs. R. F. Robson

I ROSETTA FRANCES BROWNBILL (Commonly known as Rosetta Frances Robson) of 19 Ampthill Square, Hampstead Road in the County of Middlesex, Widow, do solemnly and sincerely declare as follows.

That I am the widow of Thomas Frederick Brownbill late of No. 19 Ampthill Square aforesaid, comedian, who during his theatrical career always adopted the name of Frederick Robson and who died on the Twelfth day of August 1864.

That I was married to the said Thomas Frederick Brownbill on the 24th day of September one thousand eight hundred and forty two at the Parish Church of St. Mary Lambeth in the County of Surrey.

That there was issue of the said marriage three children only named Frederick, Frances and Edwin May, and the latter was born on the 12th day of January one thousand eight hundred and fifty five, but his birth was never registered nor was he ever christened but he has always gone and is known by the name of 'Edwin May Robson' and he is now in the twenty fifth year of his age.

That my Husband from the year one thousand eight hundred and fifty to the year one thousand eight hundred and sixty one or thereabouts did not reside under the same roof with me on account of his provincial engagements and for various other reasons which I need not here state, but he visited me from time to time at my home where my Children were, on an average of about three times a month which resulted in the birth of our son Edwin May on the Twelfth day of January one thousand eight hundred and fifty five.

My Husband returned home to me in the year 1861 and continued to live with me and our three children until his death. He always recognised Edwin May as his Son and he has never denied that he was our lawful child nor did any reason exist for his doing so.

That I make this Declaration for two reasons firstly, because it has been alleged by certain mischievous persons that because my husband was absent from home at the time of the birth of our child the said Edwin May, he was not the lawful child of my said husband; and secondly because my son the said Edwin May Robson has deemed it necessary to style himself as 'the Nephew

137

of the late Frederick Robson, Comedian', in order to distinguish himself from his Brother who is also an Actor and who advertises himself as 'the son of the late Frederick Robson'.

And lastly I declare that the said Edwin May Robson is the lawful son of my late husband Thomas Frederick Brownbill and myself. And I make this solemn declaration conscientiously believing the same to be true and by virtue of the provisions of an Act made and passed in the sixth year of the Reign of His late Majesty King William the fourth entitled 'An Act to repeal an Act of the present Session of Parliament and entitled An Act for the more effectual abolition of Oaths and Affirmations taken and made in various Departments of the State and to substitute Declarations in lieu thereof and for the entire suppression of voluntary and extra judicial Oaths and Affidavits and to make other provisions for the abolition of unnecessary Oaths'.

ROSETTA FRANCES BROWNBILL

Declared at No. 6 New Inn, Strand in the
County of Middlesex this 8th day of
December 1879. Before me
        John Arch Stuart
A Commissioner to administer Oaths in the Supreme
Court of Judicature.

Declaration 2

I MARIA BAILEY of No. 14 Church Grove Lewisham in the County of Kent Widow do solemnly and sincerely declare as follows —

1. Many years ago I went as Housemaid into the service of the late Mr. Frederick Robson who then resided at Kennington Green. His family consisted of himself and his two children Frederick and Frances. His wife was not living with him.
2. Early in the year one thousand eight hundred and fifty nine Mr. Robson removed to No. 19 Ampthill Square and I accompanied him and his family.
3. While residing at No. 19 Ampthill Square I on one occasion obtained by Mr. Robson's direction a post office order for the sum of about two pounds and sent it to a Mrs. Brownbill at an address he gave me and who he said had asked him to send the amount I forget the address to which I sent the order but it was somewhere at Hackney.
4. On another occasion I was sent to the address in Hackney and there I saw a person who said she was Mrs. Brownbill and with her was a little boy about six or seven years of age with hair inclined to be carrotty Mrs. Brownbill told me he was her nephew and his name was Edwin May.
5. Some time after this Mr. Robson was ill and Mrs. Brownbill came to the house at Ampthill Square and saw Mr. Robson in the Drawing-room

and some few months subsequently she came again and remained and Mr. Robson and his Wife the said Mrs. Brownbill then lived together. She did not bring the said Edwin May with her and down to the time at which I left Mr. Robson's service Edwin May did not appear.

6. I was married from Mr. Robson's on the twenty first day of January one thousand eight hundred and sixty two and then went to live at Carshalton in Surrey Mrs. Brownbill had come to reside at 19 Ampthill Square in the previous summer.

7. I saw Mr. Robson occasionally up to the time of his death. He and his family came to Carshalton sometimes and they would then call on me Edwin May was sent to me to stay for a holiday several times He always called Mr. Robson Uncle and Mrs. Robson Aunt and Mrs. Brownbill always spoke of him as her Nephew and in that relationship he was always known in the family.

8. I last saw Mrs. Brownbill in October one thousand eight hundred and seventy five when she called on me at Peckham where I was then living. She mentioned Edwin May and said he was doing very well as an Actor.

And I make this solemn declaration conscientiously believing the same to be true and by virtue of the Statutory Declarations Act 1835.

MARIA BAILEY

Declared at No. 167 Westminster Bridge
Road Lambeth in the County of London this
24th day of October 1895. Before me

GEO^e WILL^m BARNARD
A Commissioner for Oaths.

Declaration 3

I ROBERT CHARLES BROOKES of No. 137 Westminster Bridge Road Lambeth in the County of London MRCS do solemnly and sincerely declare as follows —

1. I have read the copy of a Statutory Declaration purporting to have been made on the 8th day of December 1879 by Rosetta Frances Brownbill Widow of Thomas Frederick Brownbill formerly of 19 Ampthill Square Hampstead Road who was better known as Frederick Robson Comedian.

2. The said Thomas Frederick Brownbill hereinafter referred to as Frederick Robson was up to the time of his death which occurred on the 12th day of August 1864 an intimate friend of my late father and from my boyhood until his death I was intimately acquainted with the said Frederick Robson and in or about the year 1861 I became acquainted with his wife the said Rosetta Frances Brownbill who had not for some time prior to that date been living with him. I was a frequent visitor at the

residence of the said Frederick Robson at 19 Ampthill Square to which house he removed in the early part of the year 1859 having bought the Lease thereof.

3. The family of the said Frederick Robson consisted of only one son Frederick Henry and one daughter Frances.

4. The said son Frederick Henry is now and has for many years been known as an actor by and under the name of Frederick Robson.

5. The said daughter Frances became my wife in the year 1871.

6. A child called Edwin about seven or eight years old resided with the family at 19 Ampthill Square and this child invariably called the said Frederick Robson Uncle and the said Rosetta Frances Brownbill Aunt.

7. The said Frederick Robson never at any time in my presence manifested the least affection for the child Edwin or recognised him as a son of his.

8. The said Frederick Robson by his Will made on the 18th day of May 1863 whereof he appointed my said late father an Executor and Trustee after giving a life interest to his Wife directed 'that his said Trustees or Trustee for the time being should hold the premises' (the trust estate) 'in trust for such of them his two children Frederick Henry Brownbill (known as Frederick Henry Robson) and Frances Brownbill (known as Frances Robson) equally or if there should be only one child then for such only child' and although there are references in other part of the said Will by his Testator to 'his said two children' and to 'his said son and daughter' there is not any mention of or allusion to or reference to or provision for any other child.

9. Edwin May Robson the Edwin to whom I refer in the 6th paragraph of this Declaration wrote to me early in the present month and enclosed to me the copy Statutory Declaration of the 8th December 1879 to which I refer in the first paragraph of this my Declaration and until then I never knew him to claim to be a son of the late Frederick Robson and the fact of the Statutory Declaration referred to having been made by the said Rosetta Frances Brownbill was not so far as I can ascertain ever made known to either my wife or her brother or to me or to my brother Walter John who was by the said Rosetta Frances Brownbill under the power reserved to her in the said Will in August 1880 appointed a new Trustee of the Will in conjunction with my late Father.

10. My wife the said Daughter of the said late Frederick Robson has read this Declaration and concurs in the Statements which I make therein. And I make this solemn declaration conscientiously believing the same to be true and by virtue of the Statutory Declarations Act 1835.

ROBERT CHARLES BROOKES

Declared at 167 Westminster Bridge
Road Lambeth in the County of London
this 24th day of October 1895.
Before me
GEO^e WILL^m BARNARD
A Commissioner for Oaths.

Declaration 4

I FREDERICK HENRY BROWNBILL better known as FREDERICK ROBSON of No. 22 Moreton Terrace St. George's Square in the County of London Comedian do solemnly and sincerely declare

1. That I have read a copy of a Declaration purporting to have been made by my mother Rosetta Frances Brownbill on the 8th day of December 1879.

2. That I never heard of this Declaration having been made by my mother until it was published in *The Stage* newspaper with a letter signed E. M. Robson written as a reply to a letter which on the 26th day of September 1895 I had written to the said newspaper.

3. I am one of the two children of the late Thomas Frederick Brownbill known more generally as Frederick Robson who died on the 12th day of August 1864. The only other child of his marriage with the said Rosetta Frances Brownbill (whose maiden name was Rosetta Frances May) was my sister Frances who became in 1871 and now is the wife of Robert Charles Brookes.

4. I was born on the 17th day of December 1843.

5. I remember as a very young child living at home with my father and mother at Kingsland and I and my sister going on a visit to my paternal grandmother in Lambeth shortly after which my father took a house in Hercules Buildings Lambeth where I and my sister lived with him but my mother never resided there. After this my father took a house on Kennington Green Lambeth to which he removed taking me and my sister with him. During our residence at Hercules Buildings and Kennington Green my father sent me and my sister to various boarding schools. In March 1859 my father purchased the lease of 19 Ampthill Square Hampstead Road and went to live there taking with him myself and my sister.

6. I was aware of my father and mother being separated my father having spoken to me upon the subject and I endeavoured to bring about a reconciliation in which eventually I succeeded and my mother came to reside at Ampthill Square with my father.

7. After my mother's return I on more than one occasion went with her to Hackney where my mother as I understood previously resided and there saw a red-headed boy who my mother called Edwin and I remember giving the boy a small gift of money on each occasion.

8. After this I was away from home for a time following my profession and when next I visited home I found this boy Edwin there as a permanent resident. He was apparently about eight or nine years of age. He addressed my father and mother always as uncle and aunt. I have in my possession two letters both dated 20 July 1878 written by the said 'Edwin' in which he mentions my mother as 'aunt' no less than seven times.

9. Until the report of the reception of Mr. Alexander's theatrical company at Balmoral appeared in the papers I never knew or heard that the said Edwin May claimed to be the son of my late father.

10. I remember the circumstances of my father making his Will the draft of

which was brought to Liverpool by Mr. Snell one of the persons named as Executors. My father was then on a starring tour at Liverpool where I also was playing. My mother and sister and Edwin May were also there and the terms of the Will were mentioned to me and to my mother Mr. Snell saying that he thought it was a proper thing to do my father being then in bad health. My mother made no comment on or objection to the Will or to the absence of any mention therein of Edwin May. And I make this solemn Declaration conscientiously believing the same to be true and by virtue of the Statutory Declarations Act 1835.

FREDERICK HENRY BROWNBILL
otherwise FREDERICK ROBSON

Declared at No. 167 Westminster Bridge
Road Lambeth in the County of London
this 24th day of October 1895
Before me

GEO^e WILL^m BARNARD

A Commissioner for Oaths.

Appendix 3

Vilikens and his Dinah[1]

Various claims have been made for the origins of 'Vilikens and his Dinah'. Clement Scott in a footnote on page 14 of *The Life and Reminiscences of E. L. Blanchard* implies that words and music were written by Blanchard himself as a boy for some private theatricals in 1839. But, although *The Wandering Minstrel* is mentioned in the playbill, there is nothing to show that the song 'Vilikens' was introduced in the play.

Peter Quennell says that Mayhew, author of *The Wandering Minstrel*, 'introduced' into it 'the celebrated cockney song' of Vilikens. But, although the first edition (1834) gives a cue for a song, no particular song is specified.[2]

Sigmund Spaeth attributes it to John Parry, on the strength of an undated edition, but James Fuld considers this to be later than the first known printing (11 November 1853).[3, 4]

Walter Rubsamen calls it 'a popular American Minstrel tune', but gives no evidence to support this curious assertion.[5]

It seems most likely that it was a traditional London street ballad of unknown origin which Robson revived in the context of *The Wandering Minstrel* in 1853, and that it was subsequently arranged for publication.

In support of this, we have Blanchard Jerrold:

It was a popular street chanson long before it was immortalised by Robson in Jem Bags.[6]

The Introduction to 'The Legend of Vilikens and his Dinah' (words only, illustrated by George Thomson), issued shortly after the first edition of the song, speaks of

. . . the romantic circumstances under which Frederick Robson became possessed of this legend, and how it was rescued from oblivion.[7]

Tantalisingly he does not tell us what these romantic circumstances were.

John Ashton, who made a special study of street ballads, says:

. . . during its run (it) was as popular as any street ballad I remember. It had been forgotten when Robson, that prince of comic actors, introduced it into the farce of the Wandering Minstrel, and it took the town by storm.[8]

John Ashton does not say at what date it was so popular as a street ballad, but, since he himself remembered it in 1888 although it had been generally forgotten, we might guess its 'run' was about 1835-1845, and allow eight years before Robson revived it in *The Wandering Minstrel* in 1853. Robson might have heard and memorised it in his young days in Lambeth, around Drury Lane, or in Islington when he was at the Grecian.

A broadside sheet of the words alone was published by James Catnach, dated 1854 in the British Library catalogue, and therefore a year later than the first printed edition of the song, from which it differs in certain particulars; it is called 'William and Dinah'. 'Go boldest daughter' becomes 'Go boldest strumpet'; and there is an extra line which would not fit the tune as we know it. The relationship of this ballad to the printed versions is obscure.

As J. W. Robinson says in an article in *Theatre Notebook:*

Street literature influenced, and was influenced by, in ways not yet described, the development of early Music Hall.[9]

Several writers (including J. C. Hotten, H. Barton Baker and Warwick Wroth) claim that Robson first sang it at the Grecian, of which I have not yet found evidence.[10] Harold Scott believed it was first performed at the Olympic, but we know Robson sang it in Dublin in February 1853. It seems strange to perform a cockney comic song before an Irish audience. M. Willson Disher alleges that Robson taught it to Toole in Dublin. This is not impossible, since the two were friends at that time, and Robson helped Toole. But Toole seems to have made no use of the song until much later.[11,12]

If the song had already been in Robson's repertoire for years, it is difficult to account for its 'taking the town by storm' when he first sang it at the Olympic.

He may well have sung it unaccompanied in the first Olympic performance. Its overwhelming success would have prompted the musical director, John Barnard, to prepare it for publication by Campbell Ransford on 11 November 1853.

The cover of this edition is largely occupied by a portrait by Augustus Butler of Jem Bags in all his rags and tatters, and bears a facsimile of Robson's signature.

Once it was published there was a rush to bring out other editions with variants in words or music. Soon it was being sung by J. L. Toole and Sam Cowell, but Robson's name is always printed first, which surely indicates that he was its first public singer.

An interesting version is Number 691 in Davidson's *Musical Treasury*, which includes Robson's spoken interludes. These were provided by E. L. Blanchard who must have memorised or noted them down on various occasions. We read in the *Life* that on 7 December 1853 Davidson called to obtain another portion; on 16 December Davidson paid him £1; on 2 January Blanchard gave him 'the signature'. This signature is presumably the 'Jem Baggs his marc' which appears on the cover, together with a crude version of the Butler portrait. The song is entitled 'The Celebrated Antediluvian and Dolefully Pathetic Legend of Willikind and his Dinah, with the melancholy and unfortunate fate of 'Ye dismal parients', and it is said to have been sung by Mr. F. Robson at the Royal Olympic Theatre (in large type), and by Mr. J. L. Toole (in smaller type).[13]

E. L. Blanchard further cashed in on the success of 'Vilikens' by producing at the Haymarket, in collaboration with Sterling Coyne, a travestie based on the story, which ran from 16 March 1854 until the end of May. But he had been preceded by Montagu Williams and F. C. Burnand, who produced a farce under the title of *Villikins and his Dinah* at the Surrey on 27 February of the same year.

These productions had only an ephemeral success, and are mentioned merely as further evidence of the sensation created by Robson's singing of the song.

Everyone was singing it. A Latin version appeared in *Diogenes* in 1854. Albert Smith wrote a French version:

C'est d'un riche marchand qui demeurait en ville
Il n'avait qu'un enfant, une très jolie fille.
Etc.

and there was also a Greek translation.

Perhaps the most surprising version was that published by Williams in 1856, with a new tune to the familiar words.

The so-called second edition of *The Wandering Minstrel*, published by John Miller — n.d. but probably 1854 — gives the words of Jem Bags' song as in the Blanchard-Davidson edition. Another so-called second edition published by Samuel French about the same time does not give the words but states that the celebrated song of 'Vilikins and his Dinah' as sung by Mr. Robson is published only by Mr. Lacy, 89 Strand, price 1s. 3d.

Words and music found their way across the Atlantic. The American Gold Rush song, 'Sweet Betsy from Pike', was set to an adaptation of the tune. Sam Cowell probably took the song with him, and a number of variants are found in manuscript form in albums.

NOTES TO APPENDIX 3

[1] The spelling varies: Villikins, Viliken, Willikind, etc. Vilikens has been used throughout, following the first edition.

[2] Introduction to a selection from *The London Poor*, London, n.d.

[3] Sigmund Spaeth: *Read 'em and weep*. London 1926.

[4] James Fuld: *The Book of World-famous Music*, New York 1971.

[5] Walter Rubsamen: 'The Ballad Burlesques and Extravaganzas', *Musical Quarterly*, October 1950.

[6] Blanchard Jerrold: *Life of Cruikshank*, London 1888.

[7] *Villikins and his Dinah;* illustrated by George Thomson, London 1854.

[8] John Ashton: *Modern Street Ballads*, London 1888.

[9] J. W. Robinson: An Amateur among Professionals, *TN*, Vol. XXVIII, p.6.

[10] J. C. Hotten in G. A. Sala: *Frederick Robson*, London 1864; H. Barton Baker: *A History of the London Stage*, London 1904; Warwick Wroth: *Cremorne and the later London Gardens*, London 1907.

[11] M. Willson Disher: *The Cowells in America*, OUP 1935.

[12] Harold Scott: *The Early Doors*, London 1946.

[13] *Notes and Queries*, 1864.

Appendix 4

The Olympic after Robson

Until September 1864 the name of Robson appeared with that of Emden on the Olympic bills, Frederick Robson having left his interest in the theatre to his wife in trust for their two children, Frederick and Frances.

But in that month W. S. Emden published a broadsheet announcing a change of lesseeship, and setting forth his grievances. Before Robson's death, Mr. G. C. Bentinck, M.P., their sleeping partner, having neglected to renew the seven-year lease had formed a Limited Liability Company with himself and Tom Taylor as directors, in which Emden but not Robson might have shares. Emden believed that he and his deceased co-lessee had been badly treated:

The wife and children of your late favourite are like myself shown the stage-door, and are privileged to sing the 'Tramp Chorus' together.

This was admirably illustrated in a caricature (unpublished) by George Thomson in the possession of Messrs. Mander and Mitchenson. Bentinck is shown smoking a Hookah, in the smoke of which appear all Robson's famous characters. Robson himself is also shown as supporting the Olympic Theatre by his talents.

In November 1864 Horace Wigan took over. Emden himself went to the St. James's as Acting Manager to Miss Herbert, and remained there some years.

Bibliography

Adams, W. D.	*A Book of Burlesque*, London, 1891.
Allen, P.	*The Stage Life of Mrs. Stirling* (Introduction by Sir Frank Benson), London, 1922.
Archer, F.	*An Actor's Notebook*, London, 1912.
Archer, W.	*Masks or Faces*, London, 1888.
Armstrong, C. F.	*A Century of Great Actors*, London, 1912.
Ashton, J.	*Modern Street Ballads*, London, 1888.
Baker, H. Barton	*History of the London Stage*, London, 1904.
Bancroft, Squire	*The Bancrofts: Recollections of 60 Years*, London, 1909.
Blanchard, E. L.	*Life and Reminiscences*, ed. Clement Scott and Cecil Howard, London, 1912.
Boase, F.	*Modern English Biography*, Truro, 1897.
Booth, M.	*English Melodrama*, London, 1965.
Burnand, F. C.	*Personal Reminiscences of the University ADC Cambridge*, London, 1880.
Cave, J. A.	*Man of the World*, ed. Robert Soutar, London, 1892.
Clinton-Baddeley, V. C.	*The Burlesque Tradition in the English Theatre*, London, 1952.
Cole, J. W.	*Life and Times of Charles Kean*, London, 1860.
Coleman, J.	*Plays and Playwrights*, London, 1888.
	50 Years of an Actor's Life, 1904.
Cook, Dutton	'Frederick Robson', *The Gentleman's Magazine*, June 1882.
Davidge, W. P.	*Footlight Flashes*, London, 1866.
Disher, M. Willson	*Victorian Song*, London, 1955.
Disher, M. Willson (ed.)	*The Cowells in America*, OUP, 1934.
Donne, W. B.	*William Bodham Donne and his Friends*, ed. Catherine Johnson, London, 1960.
Douglas, James	*Theodore Watts-Dunton*, London, 1904.
Ellis, S. M. (ed.)	*A Mid-Victorian Pepys* (Letters and Memoirs of Sir William Hardman), London, 1923.
Fleetwood, F.	*Conquest*, London, 1953.
Goldberg, I.	*The Story of Gilbert and Sullivan*, New York, 1935.
Goodman, W.	*The Keeleys*, London, 1895.
Goodwin, N. C.	*Nat Goodwin's Book*, Boston, 1917.
Hicks, Seymour	*Twenty-four Years of an Actor's Life By Himself*, London, 1910.
Hollingshead, J.	*My Lifetime*, London, 1895.
Howard, Diana	*London Theatres and Music Halls*, Library Association, 1970.
Hutton, Joseph	*J. L. Toole, chronicled by Himself*, London, 1892.
Hutton, Lawrence and Matthews, J. Brandon	*Actors and Actresses of Great Britain and the United States*, London, 1886.
James, Henry	*A Small Boy and Others*, London, 1911.
Lacy, W.	'Random Recollections', *Routledge's Annual*, 1879
Levey, R. M. and O'Rourke, J.	*Theatre Royal, Dublin*, 1880.

Lewes, G. H. and Forster, J.	*Dramatic Essays*, London, 1912.
Mackinnon, A.	*The Oxford Amateurs*, London, 1910.
Mander, R. and Mitchenson, J.	*The Lost Theatres of London*, London, 1968.
Marston, Westland	*Our Recent Actors*, Vol. II, London, 1888.
Morley, H.	*Diary of a London Playgoer*, London, 1891.
	Journal of a London Playgoer, 1851-1866, London, 1866.
Morley, M.	*Margate and its Theatres*, London, 1966.
Newton, H. Chance	*Idols of the Halls*, London, 1928.
Nicoll, A.	*A History of English Drama*, Vol. V, Cambridge, 1962.
Nicholson, R.	*The Lord Chief Baron*, London, 1966.
Peile, K.	*Candied Peel*, London, 1931.
Pemberton, T. Edgar	*The Birmingham Theatre*, Birmingham and London, 1888.
Periodicals and Press	*Birmingham Daily Post*
	Daily Telegraph
	The Era
	The Era Almanach
	Freeman's Journal, Dublin
	Illustrated London News
	Illustrated Sporting News
	Kent Herald
	Kentish Observer
	The Mask
	Morning Chronicle
	Observer
	Scotsman, Edinburgh
	Sunday Times
	Tallis's Theatrical Musical Fine Art Literary and General Family Newspaper
	The Times
	The Train
Planché, J. R.	*Recollections and Reflections*, 2 vols., London, 1872.
Pulling, C.	*They were Singing*, London, 1952.
Reynolds, H.	*Minstrel Memories*, London, 1928.
Rice, E. le Roy	*Monarchs of Minstrelsy*, New York, 1911.
Ritchie, J. E.	*About London*, London, 1860.
Robinson, H. Crabb	*The London Theatre*, edited Eiluned Brown, STR, London, 1966.
Rowell, George	*Queen Victoria goes to the Theatre*, London, 1978.
Russell, W. Clark	*Representative Actors*, London, 1870.
Sala, G. A.	Article in *The Train*, *A Sketch of Frederick Robson* (originally appeared in *Atlantic Monthly*), Introduction by J. C. Hotten, London, 1864.

Scott, C.	*From 'The Bells' to 'King Arthur'*, London, 1897. *The Drama of Yesterday and To-day*, 2 vols., London, 1899.
Scott, H.	*The Early Doors*, London, 1946.
Sherson, E.	*London's Lost Theatres of the 19th century*, London, 1925.
Sims, G. R.	*My Life*, London, 1917.
Stedman, Dr. J.	*Gilbert before Sullivan*, London, 1969.
Strauss, G. L. M.	*Reminiscences of an Old Bohemian*, London, 1880.
J. L. Toole	*Reminiscences of J. L. Toole*, chronicled by Joseph Hutton, London, 1892.
Warrack, Lou	*Theatre Unroyal*, Nottingham, 1974.
Whyte, F.	*Actors of the Century*, 1898.
Wittke, C.	*Tambo and Bones*, Durham, N.C., 1930.
Wroth, W.	*Cremorne and the later London Gardens*, London, 1907.

Index

151